T0115001

Tap into Miracles

A Reminder

Rania Lababidy

BALBOA.
PRESS

A DIVISION OF HAY HOUSE

Balboa Press books may be ordered through booksellers or by contacting:

Balboa Press
A Division of Hay House
1663 Liberty Drive
Bloomington, IN 47403
www.balboapress.com
1 (877) 407-4847

Because of the dynamic nature of the Internet, any web addresses or links contained in this book may have changed since publication and may no longer be valid. The views expressed in this work are solely those of the author and do not necessarily reflect the views of the publisher, and the publisher hereby disclaims any responsibility for them.

The author of this book does not dispense medical advice or prescribe the use of any technique as a form of treatment for physical, emotional, or medical problems without the advice of a physician, either directly or indirectly. The intent of the author is only to offer information of a general nature to help you in your quest for emotional and spiritual well-being. In the event you use any of the information in this book for yourself, which is your constitutional right, the author and the publisher assume no responsibility for your actions.

Any people depicted in stock imagery provided by Thinkstock are models, and such images are being used for illustrative purposes only. Certain stock imagery © Thinkstock.

Printed in the United States of America.

ISBN: 978-1-4525-8467-6 (sc)
ISBN: 978-1-4525-8468-3 (hc)
ISBN: 978-1-4525-8469-0 (e)

Library of Congress Control Number: 2013918513

Balboa Press rev. date: 11/13/2013

I dedicate this book to you!
May the words inspire you to live your
most magnificent life.

"At the centre of your being you have the answer;
you know who you are and you know what you want."

Lao Tse

Contents

My Inspiration

"Only passions, great passions,
can elevate the soul to great things."

Denis Diderot

We are all born with a very unique purpose to our life.

As children, we are intuitive. We know what feels good and what doesn't. We are naturally drawn to certain things and people. If we encourage this sense of self and help it grow and develop, we will be guided to our most enchanted life journey. Every answer we need is within us. How many times have we listened to our intuition by acting on an out of the blue idea, and discovered that it had steered us in exactly the right direction at precisely the right moment. That is the power of intuition. The sooner we are in sync with our higher purpose, the sooner our souls are fulfilled and our creativity can soar. In that state of utter flow and satisfaction, we are maximum productive, maximum prosperous and maximum peaceful. And the world is all the better with us in it.

This book started off as a book for those with children in their lives—parents, teachers, caregivers, aunts/uncles, godparents and many more. It was my answer to "I wish children came with a manual." Over the years, I have often been asked for advice. Whilst working with children, I realised a lot of the questions were similar and when asked how, I wanted to recommend so many books. I think in books but that's a whole other conversation! My work gathered some of the best known theories and research, adding practical and educational advice. So the "children's" book was pretty much written in 2009. For some reason, I hesitated about sending it out into the world. Clearly, there was more that I needed to experience before its publication. So a few years later, my ideas expanded into the adult world and my energy was moving me to spread the message. Essentially, my intuition led me to widen the audience since who we all are begins in childhood. To truly tap into our intuitive power, we must unravel all that we've added on since. It's a journey back to love. Carl Jung observed that "We cannot change anything until we accept it." And sometimes, it takes tracing it a few steps back to fully understand. Children come into the world filled with love and kindness, trusting life, moving towards what feels good, drawn to beauty and nature. This is who we all really are.

"Childhood constitutes the most important element in an adult's life"

Dr. Maria Montessori has been a huge inspiration for me as a person and as an educator. She seems to have been ahead of her time in everything from environmentalism to the spirit within. She believed that children are here to teach us the better way. "The child is endowed with unknown powers, which can guide us to a radiant future. If what we really want is a new world, then education must take as its aim the development of these hidden possibilities." She was nominated for the Nobel Peace Prize, receiving a total of six nominations. I am a Montessorian by training and I cannot imagine a better educational system for children. In fact, I cannot imagine a healthier approach than her ultimate respect for the child. I believe that every mother, father, teacher, caregiver and anyone with children in their life ought to discover her more in depth. I say this here because I include a lot of Montessori ideas and suggestions in this book, but it is by no means a complete acknowledgement of her brilliant work. For those interested in delving further, I include some of her own writing in the *Inspiring Books* section and examples of successful Montessori alumni like the Google founders!

Montessori

Dr. Maria Montessori was the first woman to attend Medical School in Italy, becoming a doctor before entering the field of education. Montessori believed the early years were integral in the child's capacity to *absorb*. This "sensitive" period would slow down after the age of six. Natural curiosities would be encouraged by educators who would open up a world of interesting works for children. A deep concentration would form the basis of a love of learning Montessori believed would accompany the child long after school. Through children's innate capacity to absorb information, as in the way a child masters his/her maternal language, so the child continues to discover and learn from the surrounding environment. Children are environmentalists at heart, and as she discovered during her years in India, many concepts from science to language may be learned in the most natural settings.

She observed that children liked order and quiet atmospheres. She felt repetition was good and encouraged a teaching style that allowed children to be choosers of their own education. By following a child's curiosities, and observing him or her, we could pave the way for further and more learning. Dr. Montessori emphasised teaching over correcting and observed that children have a sense of dignity and appreciate lessons in life. She once taught an entire classroom the art of blowing one's nose, to which the children applauded!

Montessori leaves the legacy of child-sized environments in most early childhood settings now. Many of the newest educational techniques stem from her focus on the child's natural rhythm. Her belief in mixing the age groups allows the younger to learn at their own pace and encourages the older to nurture those who are still learning—the children become the teachers! Children closer in age and thinking learn best from each other. Dr. Montessori concluded that children were sent to teach us the values of compassion and kindness. Children are born in the most decent state. If we truly believe in seeking peace in the world, then we must nurture and encourage these pure souls whose days we are privileged to share.

Higher Purpose

Children have come a long way from the period of being seen and not heard. Jean-Jacques Rousseau was the first to point out that there was such a thing as childhood. Many since then have acknowledged not only the importance of childhood in itself, but also the presence of spirit at that early magical time in one's life. It is as if children are born into the world as developed souls, full of love and wisdom and goodness. They are ready and eager to help others, they are naturally loving and gentle. They feel happy in nature, they are curious to discover. Children want to learn. Montessori observed that "Through some human instinct children would rather acquire knowledge than be engaged in senseless play."

There are natural curiosities and there is order to the learning, as in Piaget's conservation work. A child is only ready at a certain time for certain information. We can respect that and accompany it. For instance, let's take a child who loves to play with cars. Cars are his big passion and we want to teach him things. How about we count the cars, and eventually subtract the cars (Maths)? How about we segment the cars by attributes (Geometry, Language, Maths))? How about we draw cars (Art)? How about we write a story about the cars (Language)? How about we discover where the cars are made (Cultural/Geography)? How about we discover how they work (Science)? Always remember that children prefer real work over play. They want to learn and feel empowered, so it is our responsibility to teach.

Maria Montessori discussed *sensitive periods* in which children are open to learning. I have been particularly interested in the language learning sensitivity but clearly, this is an accompaniment to all the other learning that also takes place during this period. Not only are children's learning curves extremely steep during the sensitive periods, the information once gathered, like muscle memory, is very long-lasting. Skills practiced and mastered during this period could be called upon at much later points in life.

Remembering

It is, in fact, a remembering. We are born naturally drawn to certain interests. Dr. Montessori called these *intrinsic interests*. As we pursue those, our life flows. Somewhere along the way, that natural intuitive calling is interrupted by the *ego* mind. We are taught to think and that thinking begins to over-ride our natural drives. As we grow up, our life sometimes feels like a performance—for teachers, peers, bosses, partners and so on. At some point, we might accomplish all the accolades that go with a successful life—the beautiful home, the designer clothes, the parties, the relationship that looks good and yet, we're not happy. It might look like we have everything, but if deep down, we are feeling a certain emptiness, *this isn't it*. Sometimes, we think when we have this or that, we will be happy. The truth is that unless we are happy before, this or that can never make us happy. That's the good news. We are responsible for our own happiness.

Blaise Pascal said *"Le coeur a ses raisons que la raison ne connait point."* Our heart will always win. We may choose to ignore it for a while, but life has its ways of getting our attention. Life begins to take things away. The list is endless but usually looks like this: health, financial, partner issues. *A Course in Miracles* likens it to babies who "scream in rage" when we take away scissors or a knife from them, yet we know that this is for their protection and healthy growth. And since life is on our side, it is also looking after us and moving us in the right direction.

A Course in Miracles

When I founded KidsMeridian in Paris, I was at the question asking stage. I had begun my journey from the mind to the heart. After a scenic walk around the Seine one day, I made my way to the English bookstore in search of a good book. As I looked through the shelves and moved some books around, Marianne Williamson's *A Return to Love* landed in my lap. I had heard of her work but when I glanced through the book, I wasn't sure that was what I was looking for. So I continued browsing . . . But her face on the cover kept calling me back. I felt drawn to the book, plus it had found me! I bought it and went home. That was my introduction to *A Course in Miracles*. Loving Marianne's work, I read all her books and listened to every audio available. I practiced her meditations and loved the prayers. Her words spoke to my soul.

I went on to discover Alan Cohen's work and the same thing happened. I read every book he wrote. By now, I realised I was truly fascinated by the concepts of *A Course in Miracles*. So after owning it for about a year, I dived in. It is a three volume work including a Text, Workbook for Students and Manual for Teachers.

A Course in Miracles was born in answer to "There must be another way." The book was written as a collaborative venture by Helen Schucman and William Thetford, professors of Medical Psychology at the Columbia University College of Physicians and Surgeons in 1965.

To me, ACIM represents a perfect summary of some of my favourite thinkers: From Socrates to Rumi to Carl Jung to Kahlil Gibran to Albert Einstein to Paulo Coelho!

Intention

"And when you want something,
all the universe conspires in helping you to achieve it."

Paulo Coelho

G nothi Seauton is the Delphic injunction "Know thyself." It is inscribed in the Temple of Apollo in Delphi. From the Ancient Egyptians to Plato to Ralph Waldo Emerson to *The Matrix*, this is the maxim. It is essentially the very beginning of the story. How simple it sounds and yet how many of us are still figuring it all out. Step by step. Day by day. Getting to know ourselves. Who are we really . . . What makes us come alive and glow from within?

Abraham Maslow observed "It isn't normal to know what we want. It is a rare and difficult psychological achievement." And that is precisely the point when our journey may begin. An intention. A moment where we examine our truth. Our deepest truest heart's desire. What do we really want?

The Ancient Greeks warned against paying too much attention to the opinions of *the multitude*. Total freedom is exactly that. Anytime we are feeling somewhat torn inside, it is because we have created a gap between who we are and what it might look like to the outside world. Who we are and what we want are our truth. They are the part of us that is linked to universal power.

Kahlil Gibran wrote "It is thy desire in us that desireth." Our truest deepest most genuine desire is life's whisper, reminding us that this is the journey we are here to experience.

So take a moment, a candle-lit moment if you like, and write down what you really really really want. Forget how impossible it might be. Just acknowledge it. Know it. Own it. And let's go from there. This is a universe of infinite possibilities. Let's tap into miracles!

The desire may change along the way. It will be fine-tuned and perfected from this day forward. The journey towards it is what our soul came here for. We have to prepare to receive it. In becoming someone who is ready for this to manifest, many layers may need to be shed. As Rumi discovered, "Your task is not to seek for love, but merely to seek and find all the barriers within yourself that you have built against it."

Life wants us to have everything we want. In fact, life's ideas for us are sometimes so much bigger and better than those we have for ourselves. But when we settle for less than what our heart truly desires, we shut down our connection to source energy and things feel rough. Anytime it feels tough, there is a lesson involved. It is the universe's way of asking us to raise our game.

We are here to live our most magnificent life. An inspired and inspiring life. It is in tapping into our truth that we reach the miraculous.

This book offers many steps. I have presented these in the order they unfolded for me. Since the idea is always about coming back to our intuitive power, we will be drawn to the steps in the sequence that is right for us. They are all interconnected and the themes will complete each other.

Intuition will guide us along and we will tap into our perfect health, our perfect wealth, our perfect love and our perfect self-expression.

We will know what passion feels like, our creative selves, and our power to be miracle magnets bringing to us our best most abundant life.

It's a very exciting journey and I am so inspired to share it with you.

I know this is the beginning of something very important . . . Enjoy!

Movement

"Go confidently in the direction of your dreams.
Live the life you have imagined."

Henry David Thoreau

As adults, we exercise to be fit and healthy. We exercise to feel good and look after our physical bodies. Exercise releases endorphins, and we feel exhilarated with vigorous energy. It not only adds fun and takes our mind off things, it is also important for the brain. Research is showing that even developed cases of Alzheimer's show a favourable response to exercise being re-introduced. Exercise is important for healthy digestion. Exercise is important for restful sleep. Exercise and movement are important, no two ways about it.

It is especially so in childhood. Dr. Maria Montessori observed that "if a child is prevented from using his powers of movement when they are ready, the child's mental development is obstructed." Children are not supposed to sit still for hours on end. It is not age-appropriate. Children need to move, to jump, to twirl for their brain to develop. When parents complain about their kids' non-stop movement "they don't stop moving" "they're jumping all the time," it is worth remembering that children come into the world as highly intuitive souls. They know what they need. And movement is something they need.

Often, when I am working with a child who is deeply concentrating, of his own volition, he will get up and move around and again, on his own, he will come right back to continue the work where he left off. For mental development, children need to physically move. It is a regular occurrence and might happen three or four times before they complete a work. It's good for them. It's more than good for them, it's a necessity for their healthy progress.

Physiologically

Physiologically, a child needs to move. His body proportion is such that movement is essential for his healthy growth. Muscles constitute the biggest part of our bodies. A newborn's legs are 32% of his height whereas for an adult the lower limbs are about half our body. At the age of three, the legs make up about 38%. Such numbers alone should be convincing of a child's natural desire to move. Standing on their short legs is quite an exercise in balance for children and they usually run to mask the difficult task of walking. Children tend to rest with their stomach on the floor and their lower legs turned upwards. They will usually raise their shoulders and stabilise on the elbows.

Children have a natural urge to coordinate their muscles for the movements to flow. This is an energy drive coming from within. We must allow them that self-discovery and the perfection they are seeking.

Practical Life

Children prefer real work to play. Getting dressed is a highly complex task for children and one that gathers both confidence and movement. Zippers, buttons, laces, safety pins—these are all serious business for a kid to master. Children are fascinated by precision. They are motivated by the order of things. Their interest in where the soap is placed and the folding of the towel are more grabbing to them than the actual process of hand-washing. So show them how to do tasks with precision, for they will copy every move. And know that if we flip our hair in the midst of a presentation, they will do that too!

Children below the age of three are fascinated by order. The correct placing of furniture in a room is of utmost importance to them and this, as an activity, encourages much movement.

Discovery

Gyms are a great setting for children to master muscle movements. Climbing, balancing, jumping, running, twirling. All the different movement possibilities encourage muscle perfection. The child is also developing spatial skills and mental planning. And he is learning socialisation skills whilst in motion. He must wait his turn. If he collides into someone, he will learn to sympathise with another's pain or sadness. We would ask the hurt child if he wanted water and the answer would unequivocally be yes. So, the responsible child would grab a glass of water for his friend and somehow everyone would be soothed. It was the magic recipe every time.

So many times, I'm standing in the supermarket queue, and I watch children looking around them, trying to access new knowledge whilst adults are busy scolding them about not touching anything, and not moving! Life is about movement. Requesting that a child stand still like a statue while we conduct our business is not natural. Children discover the world through movement, through touching, feeling, smelling, tasting. They are merely exploring.

$E = mc2$

Energy equals matter moving forward. Albert Einstein discovered that "nothing happens until something moves." To move is to feel. The Chinese express it as moving Chi or energy around the body. Emotion is to create movement. Love, anger, fear are all meant to incite us to move forward—either towards what we love or away from what makes us angry. Even fear is about proceeding with caution.

Exercise releases beta endorphins. The Vagus nerve which is essential for our parasympathetic nervous system to feel relaxed, to feel good, is activated through breathing fully. This happens when we exercise and when we meditate. Exercise takes us forward physically and mentally and meditation takes us forward emotionally and spiritually.

Our Heart's Desire

Our deepest truest heart's desire is the starting point. It is, in fact, our point of power. When we acknowledge what it is that our soul yearns for and take even the most minor step towards it, life comes in and supports us every step of the way. Sometimes the desire is felt unconsciously. As in, we're living our life getting on with it but deep in our being, we know this isn't it. That inner stirring also gets things moving. Much of the time, some drama is incurred. We lose the job, the relationship, our money or we might even get ill. Life's options for getting us moving are many.

Just know that when consciously or unconsciously, our soul yearns for something else, life will move us in that direction. So when it looks like a mess just when you've declared your deepest truest heart's desire, accept that as part of the journey. Things have to change to move us along. In fact, do more than that. Embrace the change. Thank it, knowing that as you move through it, focused on what it is you really want, every step of the way will heal what needs healing and prepare you to be the person ready to receive. Winston Churchill said "if you're going through hell, keep going." That is the truth. It might look like hell but if we're open to its gifts, the gold will emerge.

We come into the world primed for our happiness and everything that contributes to that. Our soul knows the plan. Sometimes, our ego takes over for a moment and we're living a life that looks good but really doesn't feel good—on any level. As we become aware of that, even a fragment of awareness, gets the ball rolling. Thomas A. Edison pointed out that "discontent is the first necessity of progress."

The First Step

"Faith is taking the first step even when you don't see the whole staircase." Martin Luther King, Jr.

Life really encourages our first step. The first step might be as simple as deciding to change the road we take to work every day, or the deli where we eat lunch. The key is to move towards what feels good. If the longer road to work is more scenic and therefore more soothing, then that's the one. If the other deli offers a better meal, that's the one. The moment we start looking after ourselves, life joins in. When we are clear on our desire, a little action goes a long way. I remember when I worked in finance, many times I would notice that when someone starts going to the gym regularly, he or she invites some big change.

It's really about making a decision, within ourselves, that something must change. And, at that point, going with the flow. My first step involved moving to NYC. I know it sounds major. Truth is though, it was very simple. I knew I needed some sort of change. My ultimate dream was to live in the midst of lavender fields in Provence. So New York City was a little from left field. I loved the Big Apple. I went there often for long weekends. I always had a good time. And my heart just wanted to be there. It was really just like that. I asked my boss if the bank would transfer me and within two weeks, the move had begun. It was so easy, so supported by the universe. I went from daily struggle, accidents and dramas, to an enchanted journey to my beloved NYC. And from there, I never looked back. Every step followed in perfect timing.

Love

"If only you could love enough
you would be the happiest
and most powerful
being in the world."

Emmet Fox

*A*ttachment is a basic need for humans. In order to develop healthily and solidly through life's stages, we need to form a bond with at least one other. For a child, the other is the significant adult in his life. This adult's presence is comforting to the child. The adult responds to him and as a result, the child feels safe in the world. Having spent about nine months in the comfort of a mother's womb, the newborn is brutally exposed to an unknown, bright and noisy world. The adult in the infant's life would ideally offer comfort, tenderness and warmth, as well as meeting the basic needs of food and hygiene. Everything that a baby needs for his first year is found in the mother's breast milk. It's as easy as that. The milk offers the nutrients and the immunity building. In fascinating work on *Igniting Intuition*, Dr Christiane Northrup points out that breast milk also contains Omega 3 or DHA, which ultimately contributes to more intelligence and higher IQ. In some countries, DHA is not added to formula milk as it is an expensive component. Breast feeding also offers a position in which the child feels body warmth and a connection, physical and emotional.

It is important to point out that the provision of food is not the ultimate goal. What the baby needs, even more than food, is the emotional and physical connection. They are in need of a reliable source of love. Psychologist Harry Harlow conducted research on baby monkeys offering two 'surrogate mothers.' One mother was made of hard wire whilst the other of terrycloth. The monkeys always went to the soft terrycloth mother, even when the hard wire one had the food!

This is what Erikson called *Hope*—the trust versus mistrust stage. After the warmth and comfort of the womb, out here in this big wide world, will my needs will be reliably met? It is a child's first experience with pain and it is his introduction to love. It is the definition of unconditional love. There are two aspects to this stage: the warmth and the reliability. The infant needs to know that the caregiver will warmly *and* reliably respond to his crying. In the absence of such attachment, the child is insecure. Harville Hendrix, PhD., suggests that the child might become a clinger if the adult has been warm but unreliable. Or the child may become a loner if the adult has been reliable but distant. It has been shown that children who lack healthy attachments tend to be devoid of empathy. Many crimes in the world are conducted by those who feel no remorse.

When adults go into therapy at a later stage in their life, much of the time it is to correct this basic unmet emotional need. It is through work with the therapist that one re-builds trust in another, and the world, and is then able to develop through the other stages.

When we find mothers exacerbated by a child who won't sleep the nights or a child who doesn't respond, it is often linked to that basic attachment issue. Through art or play therapy, we are able to observe the missing link. With remedial work, where the adult corrects this and reconnects with the child, the child returns to a state of peacefulness.

Babies who sleep too much or who cry upon waking might be giving us an indication that they are not enjoying their waking hours. They have come out from a warm, comfortable, soothing environment into a world that does not feel good and safe to them. Dr. Maria Montessori noted that these babies were preferring to regress back to their state within the womb.

It is at this stage that a baby first realises that he might be a separate entity and it is up to the adults to offer him an enjoyable experience of interconnectedness. For ultimately, life is interconnected. We are not separate. We are here to care and be cared for. We are meant to work together towards a better world. We are, at our core, in sync with nature and part of the whole. We are connected to others and to life itself. We are born interconnected, naturally caring for others and our surroundings.

Love

The way we love our children will become their benchmark. By being loved unconditionally, we know what true love feels like. Healthy relationships are interdependent. They are respectful. Healthy relationships empower and strengthen us. They bring out the best in us. They propel us to be the best we can be. Difficult relationships in adulthood usually replicate the kind of love that is familiar to us from our childhood. A distant or a mildly disapproving love can haunt us. When children know what a healthy relationship feels like, they will strive for no less than that.

Risk

Life is risk-taking. Everyday, we go out and live. If we never took risks, we would stay in a very limited cocoon— our comfort zone. We need to stretch that comfort zone a little every day to be truly growing. Abraham Maslow remarked that "Life is an ongoing process of choosing between safety (out of fear and need for defence) and risk (for the sake of progress and growth). Make the growth choice a dozen times a day."

That's what we need to offer children. Freedom to choose their life, to construct it themselves, all the time knowing that we believe in them no matter what. From the unconditional support we receive from our loved ones, we develop a core that begins to believe that we can handle it all. Once we are aware that we can do it, life flows because we operate from a space of love and not fear. What we fear always comes back to test us. In fact, by fearing, we bring about our fears. The goal is to operate from love so we may flow.

Will

In the old days, children were seen as wicked or rebellious for disobeying. It is important to point out that the exercise of will is a rather precious gift. It is easy for adults to break a child's will and have him obey. But how much more satisfying to have a child choose to follow instructions out of respect for the person giving them. Before the age of three, a child has not mastered his conscious actions and often, he is incapable of responding to the request. He is purely not ready yet. He is not disobeying out of rebellion but rather out of a lack of ability to control his actions. Sometimes, he may perform the task one day only to fail the next. He is still practicing. From the age of three onwards, he becomes more in control of himself and upon explanations, he will take in the reasonings. Even though we sometimes feel like we are repeating the same thing over and over again, when the response does take place from a point of consciousness, it is far more satisfying and coherent, and respectful of you.

Trust

It is important to assume responsibility for one's life. Johann Wolfgang von Goethe summed it up perfectly, "As soon as you trust yourself, you will know how to live." We are not someone else's higher power. We need to focus on our own lessons and trust that others have their own life to live. That way, no one is to blame. Not even ourselves. The lessons are part of the learning. There are no mistakes, only opportunities for growth.

The more trusted one is, the more we excel and operate from a responsible place.

Home

For all intents and purposes, and in the absence of atypical or regressive issues, children are born with an internal drive toward independence. The child is a joyful being, always enthusiastic. Dr. Montessori says the child is "in love" with his world! And nature is directing the pace. His senses are his introduction to the world. Even though still motionless, his mind is alert, absorbing his environment through the senses. His eyes are discovering this world. He is actively looking for impressions. These impressions are becoming ingrained in his psyche. "Children become like the things that they love."

A child falls in love with his early surroundings. He looks around and without judgment, loves where he comes from. Doctors have frequently found that after treatment options are exhausted, just sending people back to the air they knew as children would cure them of all ills. This is how important our home setting is. It is our repair point in life. It will be with us forever.

Relationships

"Lovers don't finally meet somewhere.
They're in each other all along."

Rumi

*P*ossibly the most difficult lesson I've had to learn in this lifetime. Here goes. I, like many girls, grew up with a Cinderella type image of our love rescuing us. That's what I always thought. Sort of like my life would start when I found him, or married him. I went to Wellesley College, Hillary Clinton's alma mater. The college mission is 'Women who make a difference.'

I go to a college that produces amazing women, women who genuinely make a difference. Madeleine Albright, Diane Sawyer, Nora Ephron, Madame Chiang Kai-shek. From campus, I head to Wall Street and over ten years later, I'm still expecting this big love of mine to rescue me to the life I really want. At some Canadian airport, with a flight delay of many hours, I finally reach a conclusion. What am I waiting for? Why don't I just get on with the life I want now.

And so, I throw in the towel on the world of finance and head back in the direction of what my heart truly came here to experience. No man on my mind, just a big passion and, at last, a life that I want.

Sure enough, that's when I meet him, this big love. And guess what, I'm ready to ditch the passion for this love. But life won't let me. *A Course in Miracles* teaches that relationships are *assignments*. Very simple concept when we get it. We meet who we need to meet to deepen our experiences, our wisdom. And the attraction is what draws us in. The work wouldn't be done if there wasn't an attraction keeping us there. Clever life!

Divine Love

We are born, part of the whole. We come into the world and detach from the divine as we take on life's lessons. And we embark on this journey to attach. As adults, this deep yearning for the 'special' relationship is in all of us. We are here to connect and without it, life feels like it's missing something. So we meet someone to whom we are attracted, and the lessons begin.

We are here to learn about unconditional love and we are here to learn about *One* love. When we love one person in a *special* way, our expectations from this *special* partner bring up all our childhood wounds and any other hurts we have also incurred along the way. Our expectations for this special love's behaviour are heightened. We're on alert to anything not quite meeting our demands. We project all our fears onto them. Big time. So here we are deeply in love whilst in a passive aggressive way, actually annoyed with them. They remind us of all our previous pain and they bring it all up again! See where it's an *assignment*—We actually have an incredible opportunity to heal those wounds with this specific person. Hence the attraction. And the assignment. That's why we've been brought together in the first place.

Notice how we tend to be attracted to people who in one way or another remind us of our childhood programming. Depressed Mum, Doting Mum, Absent Dad, Ambitious Dad . . . Catch the similarities? You will now. It's our way of taking off from where the pain left off and believing that this one (quite similar) subconsciously chosen will get it right. They'll love us the way we need to be loved. Chances are quite slim though since we've chosen the same character.

Take the boy who had a socialite Mum who was too busy and perhaps just not very maternal. He falls in love with a total socialite in the hope that this one will become more loving and maternal through the relationship, the marriage even. Or the girl who chooses a total workaholic, just too busy for her with his life. She's back to square one, priority number 10 on the list! How are these people going to heal an old wound? Their love is familiar, so we are attracted but unless we are consciously bringing up our hurts to be healed, we're going to spiral from one attraction to another, different faces same relationship.

Think of the pressure we place on one person to meet our every expectation from previous wounds to future desires. Quite a heavy burden. Since all communication takes place at the mind level, we can feel when we are disappointing someone. Even if they are pretending all is fine, the energy behind that says it's not. It's never about the words or the actions, it's about that feeling.

A Course in Miracles explains how *special* is actually the downfall of a relationship. So what helps? Releasing attachment. All attachment. No agenda, no demands, just love. "I love you exactly as you are. You are free to live the experiences you have come here to have." This, of course, does not mean we have to be doormats and accept everything. Absolutely the contrary. Since love begins with us, and expands, we are first and foremost true to ourselves. And love sometimes means walking away. Interestingly though, in releasing others to live the life that is right for them, something amazing usually happens. The energy is free again and we want the other to be happy.

Soulmate or a Match?

> *"My first glimpse of you was not in truth the first. The hour in which our hearts met confirmed in me the belief in Eternity and in the immortality of the Soul."* Khalil Gibran

We recognise soul mates at the deepest level of our being—Soul recognition. It was in the plan that we would meet. They feel familiar, déjà-vu. They move us along our journey to our best self. They consume us, challenge us and reveal to us our truth, our strength, our power. They open our hearts to all the love within us, our capacity to love and go on loving.

Our match feels different. It's an attraction that is beyond us. While the soulmate takes us on a journey to our best self, the match may bring out the worst in us. In a way, we need to first find our power before we can be properly matched. It is our attracting, our magnetising our truth back to us. We are now in a position to transcend—a love to take us to the next level of our physical presence.

While the soulmate takes us spiritually to places we'd forgotten about and reminds us who we are and why we are here; our match might be our partner in this lifetime to complete what we came here to do.

And sometimes, our soulmate is also our match.

Let me elaborate

They say that in every relationship there is a lover and a loved one. We know that, we've probably lived on both ends of that equation at different times. We've also watched others in relationship with that dichotomy taking place.

My theory states that we start out on one end and that unless we shift ends during the relationship, perhaps many times, the union will never be fully satisfying to either party.

Say the lover starts off feeling like they met their soulmate and the soulmate is delighted with the love, the attention, the uplifting. Unless the lover gently focuses on offering all that love back to herself (or himself), the partnership will remain lofty. And the soulmate might even abuse that love.

Let me emphasise that I'm not talking about playing games here. I am talking about a genuine self-love that must emerge in both parties fully during the relationship, for it is only from that place that we are in a position to offer true love. Love without agenda. Love that supports, encourages, admires, respects and excites. We have to have our own dance going on with life in order to be in a healthy relationship. All else is needy love which, at its core, is heavy and unappealing.

Unconditional Love

Victor Hugo said, "To love another person is to see the face of God." God is love and love is God. At the deepest level of our being, we are longing to know how to love as God loves. Fully, completely, unconditionally. When our heart is wide open and we are loving in that way, it becomes close to impossible to distinguish loving someone from connecting with the divine. We are in love with life itself. That kind of love is life-changing. So very powerful. It is, in fact, our road to the miraculous. It is the energy of oneness.

Rumi explains "There is a kiss we long for our entire lives." Eventually, we come to understand that what we are really yearning for is a connection with the divine in us. No one on the outside can ever fill that gap. As we develop spiritual practices that bring us closer to that love, we feel filled up from the inside out. And how much more attractive is that? We want to be around that energy.

Finding fault in others is tiring. It is the quickest way to disturb our peace of mind. When our prayer is for the other's happiness regardless of our presence in the equation, we feel lighter, happier. Just keeping an image of them with a big smile on their face does the trick! Whenever something in their behaviour disturbs us, we go back to that image. It is such a sure way of recalibrating the energy. Wishing for their happiness is a direct route to bringing about our own happiness. Miracle territory.

Soul Family

When in the presence of soul family, we feel energised, inspired, uplifted, electric and divinely irresistible! We feel understood and loved. You know, the people with whom time flies and our heart sings. Some members of our family usually feel this way. They joined us from the beginning and they are a part of our life. Others we encounter along the journey. We recognise them right away. They feel so good to us, on every level. We love being with them and we love who we are when we are with them. Our eyes twinkle. We feel so alive, so courageous, so happy. They believe in us and their message is "Go for it!"

We really want to try to spend as much time as possible with this group.

Tyrants

A tyrant might be an ex, a parent, a child, a boss, a colleague. Usually if we haven't completely made peace with one tyrant and we are trying to just distance ourself from the situation at hand, we will come across a replacement tyrant—Same issue, different person. Tyrants are great because they help perfect us. It is easy to love the loveable. They feel good on every level. How much more of a challenge it is to be open-hearted with those getting on our nerves. But that's really it, isn't it? Unconditional love in practice.

What if every single person we come across in our lifetime is part of a grand plan? What if there is an amazing vision for our life and in order to get there—*perfect health, perfect wealth, perfect love and perfect self-expression*—We have to pay attention to the signs. What if every single person and encounter hold a piece of this message? And what if the only way we might access that important information, is by seeing them through beautiful eyes . . .

And someone is *So* getting on our nerves and we wish we just didn't have to deal with them. Well here goes. People are in our lives for different reasons. Maybe we can help them, maybe they can help us and maybe we just have some soul work to do together. Whatever the purpose, life communicates a lot via people.

Here's the strategy, we focus on everything we love about them. There's always something. Might be their dimple or the colour of their lipstick. Whatever it is. In finding the beauty, we are open to hearing the message. And remember, all strange behaviour is usually just a cry for love.

Only Love is Real

All action stems from fear or love. Fear brings about insecure behaviour, love connects us to source energy. We feel at one with the world when we love. When we love ourselves, we can never hurt another or the planet. And at the end of our life, the only thing we will take with us is that love.

A friend once told me that she thought school was a horrible world. I, being in education, obviously asked her to explain. She said that she sends her gentle daughter to school where the little girl gets bullied, pushed and shoved, even hit sometimes by other children. The way I see it is, it's a good opportunity to learn socialisation skills. Without experience, one would never know how to interact with others. The unfortunate thing with all this is, the children who are learning certain behaviours at home. They then show up at school and practice what they see their families do: shout, hit, scream, be rude, sulk, ignore and more. Children watch us very closely. They watch our actions and our reactions. They watch our manners, our style and they model themselves on us. Not what we say necessarily, but what we do for sure. So, watch your actions. Be a person of integrity. Be someone of your word, be honest, be kind, be good. We can't ask our children to be something we are not. We certainly can't expect that.

At-One-ment

> "Everything that irritates us about others can lead us to an understanding of ourselves." Carl Jung

In spirituality, we often hear "We are One." At first, this concept is quite intense to understand. One of my favourite ways of unravelling all this is through the mirror of life. Just look around—right now—at who is in your life. What you love most about them is in you. And what irritates you most about them is also you (your shadow or disowned self).

Basically, it goes like this: *If you spot it, you've got it!* So anyone who is pushing our buttons is actually a very important teacher in our life.

Enlightenment is reaching a state of peace regardless of the situation. A place where we completely trust that whatever is happening in our life is *exactly* what is supposed to be happening. And whoever is with us is *exactly* who is supposed to be with us. And what we are here to do is *exactly* what is being asked of us at that moment.

Our shadow is very powerful in our life because either we use it or it uses us. Either we bring it to the light and let it spread light or we keep it in the dark because we absolutely don't want to deal with it . . . and it finds its own voice in destroying us. Think of the pristine wife, very judgmental of what's appropriate and what's not; and behind the scenes, she's off having a wild affair. Her shadow is her sexy side which she is so busy negatively pointing out in others whilst her own out of control behaviour eats away at her family life and eventually her health.

Our shadow is usually that of which we are most ashamed. Something we feel is so unacceptable in us. Ironically, as Rumi said, "The wound is where the Light enters you." And when this darkness is brought to the light and used in service to the world, it can be our biggest gift and contribution.

When sexy is turned around it might contribute to a creative drive that empowers women to feel hot, fun and passionate about their life. Not settling for anything less than that. And we all know that living a passionate life uplifts everyone we meet. That energy is the energy that creates empires.

The mirror of life is wonderful because we can use it all day every day to gage where we're at. Who inspires you? You've got it too. Who is irritating? Bring the shadow to the light. One of my shadows was "harsh". *Harsh* people kept popping up in my life as I continued to try to be my most gentle self. I had the *harsh* family member, the *harsh* boyfriend, the *harsh* best friend, the *harsh* colleague, the *harsh* client and more . . . Until I figured all this out. It turned out that this *harsh* shadow of mine wasn't so bad. I quite liked the fact that it got things done when sometimes others were dragging their feet. Essentially, I decided that *harsh* was actually very helpful and decided to rename it "tough cookie." And let me tell you, I'm a big fan of tough cookie me. She gets things done, she doesn't accept less than she knows she deserves, and she really uses that energy to do good and inspire others to live their truth and own their power.

Carl Jung also said that "If there is anything that we wish to change in the child, we should first examine it and see whether it is not something that could better be changed in ourselves." I have a friend who is hugely conscientious, productive and driven. She has two daughters. One is just like her, an energy bubble. And the other is dreamy, likes to take her time, enjoys nature and gentleness. Type B in personality, she will live to be a hundred. Very relaxed and relaxing to be with.

Unless you are Type A and thinking, "What is up with this kid?" See what I mean about the mirror of life?! My friend is concerned that her daughter might be "lazy." She is essentially projecting her shadow onto the little girl. The little girl is perfect. And my friend is too, once she brings her *lazy* shadow to the light. My friend loves to be around the house reading but feels guilty doing that—She feels she is not using her time productively. By substituting the term *relaxed* for *lazy*, both her daughter's behaviour and her disowned self would be heading to the light. Her daughter might be a poet in the making. And I bet my friend is a writer whose inspiration would be hugely tapped into through *relaxed* moments at home reading. Writers are readers. They read a lot. A lot.

As Aldous Huxley wrote, "There is only one corner of the universe you can be certain of improving and that's your own self." So the mirror of life is brilliant that way. Pick out your disowned selves. Make peace with them. Bring them to the light and see where that journey takes you.

In the end, it's not about tolerating all the different parts of ourselves, it's about embracing every part of ourselves. In our darkness, shines our light. The light we are here to spread.

Creativity

"You can only become truly accomplished
at something you love.
Don't make money your goal.
Instead pursue the things you love doing
and then do them so well
that people can't take their eyes off of you."

Maya Angelou

*W*e are all born creative. It is within us all and part of us. The more in touch we are with our truth, the more creativity can filter through us. Life is waiting for us to be in sync with ourselves to channel through us the most glorious creations. This is why so many artists, musicians, even writers sometimes cannot clearly explain where their genius came from. It was just there, their spirit took over and the work was done.

That spirit is our intuition, our connection to truth and to source energy essentially. When you trust yourself and what draws and attracts you, you will flow towards your creativity. You will loose all concept of time. You will be creating so wholly and naturally. You will be contributing to the world the best that is in you. This is your excellence. It might be a mathematical formula and it might be the most delicious risotto recipe. The point is that you are adding beauty and love into the world. This is essentially why we are here.

Concentration, flow, creativity. They are all big words and very important. The first time a child concentrates on a work is the beginning of it all. Dr Maria Montessori called that "Normalisation." I call it creativity. It is that utter fascination with whatever it is, that heralds the beginning of learning. You are now en route. All you need is encouragement, nourishment and support. Flow is the passage of time without one realising it. Sometimes, I'm so absorbed in what I'm doing that I forget to eat! Creativity is the process and/or the result of that work. It is important to emphasise that the process is just as important as the result. Many highly creative people never even begin to tackle their brilliance as they are too focused on the end result. The key is to begin. Let the universe guide you on the path. If there is something inside of you calling, just start. And finish if you can. So much wonderful work is 'almost done' and therefore inaccessible to the world. Finish it so it makes it into the world and guides and inspires those it is meant to reach.

Encouragement is vital. No one exists in a vacuum. Sometimes, we need to pull away to figure ourselves out, but ultimately, we are all in this together. We are born to connect. To love and be loved. It is not our place to judge or criticise, manipulate or influence. The best we can do is be there, with love and support. Stephen Covey calls it "empathic listening." This is the most essential tool. By listening from the heart, we will be empowering others to figure things out for themselves. We all know what the right answer is for us. It comes from deep within us, from our intuition. So many times, we ourselves, or the influences around us, sabotage that intuition with rationalisation and too much thinking. The point is to return to core, back to what feels good. Following the energy is the way.

Our main purpose in life is to create. We are here to create. Whenever we feel stuck or in a rut, it is because the vital energy of creation is stagnant. We need to create to have energy. It's not the other way around. Creating satisfies the soul and more inspiration keeps coming at us to help us continue and elaborate on our creation. God, the great Creator, wants us to create and encourages us in our success. We have to just do what we love and the energy will keep flowing through us.

Multiple Intelligences

Traditional schooling has tended to focus and praise language and mathematics at the expense of all else. Howard Gardner, Harvard Graduate School of Education and visiting Professor at NYU's Steinhardt School of Culture, Education, and Human Development, has been promoting multiple intelligences for a while. His theory states that we have natural intelligences. Some children are particularly good at languages, whilst others are perhaps more musical. Remember, Mozart was clearly musical from the age of three! A spatial child, for instance, would be able to figure his way back if left in downtown Boston . . . Interpersonal skills are what make great politicians, psychologists and teachers. Of course, we may have several intelligences that are particularly noteworthy. Linguistic, Logico-Mathematical, Musical, Spatial, Bodily Kinesthetic, Interpersonal and Intrapersonal.

Children are naturally drawn to that about which they are curious. Eventually, this may also prove to be what they are actually good at. So, follow the child. Let the child show you what he needs to learn and master. Dr. Maria Montessori believed we must let the uniqueness unfold. Basically, we are here to direct the interest, not the child.

A Guide to Creativity

"An infant walks to perfect his own proper functions, and consequently his goal is something creative within himself." Maria Montessori

At about the age of one, the child places his foot flat on the ground. He is able to make his first steps, if helped. A few months later, he is en route to walking independently.

Movement allows the child to understand his environment. Here, the senses play their role. The brain directs and the child uses his willpower to practice and perfect movements. The child is essentially learning to coordinate himself. At this stage, almost any movement can be learned. Through movement, the child's personality begins to surface. Every being has a unique way of doing things. We all learn to write but our handwriting is our own. The child is directed, beyond his conscious, to the movements that will serve his higher purpose.

Exploration stage

This is when a child begins to explore the world. The more securely attached the child is, the more comfortable he will be. He will take risks knowing that he can always look back and count on his primary caretaker being there. A child who is insecurely attached at this toddler stage will explore hesitantly and might not develop enough willpower and persistence.

In Harlow's experiment discussed earlier, monkeys who came into an unfamiliar room with their cloth "mother" clung to her at first, and then slowly began to explore the room. Every once in a while, they would return to the cloth mother. Monkeys who were placed in a room without the cloth mother would run around crying and screaming, unable to focus on anything. Monkeys who were placed in the room with the wire mother behaved in the same way as those placed in the room without a mother. When the cloth mother returned, the monkeys would cling to her instead of exploring, highlighting the preference for comfort to exploration.

This is why it is so vital for children to form healthy attachments first. This way, when they are feeling comfortable in the world, they will explore and they will persevere. They know that they are loved. Risking self-discovery is do-able. When life is scary and untrustworthy, every risk takes on the hugest proportion. The child is living and operating from a stressful state. Always unsure. His basic need for comfort and trust in the world is missing.

Identity

This stage coincides with pre-school. This is when the child begins to feel a sense of accomplishment. It is important to encourage and support his efforts. If he is shamed at this stage, he will begin to hide parts of himself. He will sense his parents approval, or not, and will cater to please them. He will begin to classify parts of himself as 'good' and 'bad'. This distinction will influence his future presentation and the sharing of himself. It would, of course, have been entirely influenced by the adults. We must remember that in allowing the child to discover every aspect of himself, he will feel comfortable with every aspect of himself. From there, he will intuitively follow what feels good to him. He will be more intrinsically drawn to certain interests. He will be curious about those and naturally successful in these areas. He will be en route to living a hugely fulfilling life.

It starts that early on. Not only from a career perspective but from a relationship perspective as well.

Our encouragement and support of every aspect of the child will help him stay authentic and true to himself. He will pursue work that feels right to his soul. Working will not feel like a chore in his life. It will be energy in, as opposed to energy out. He will discover himself through the relationships he encounters along that path. He will be comfortable with himself. As the French say, he will be "bien dans sa peau." He will literally be good in his skin. He will be honest since he has nothing to hide. He will be himself living a life of truth. Needless to say, this will be a great help not only in choosing his future career path but also his closest circle of friends and relationships. Intimacy is ultimately the ability to share every aspect of oneself.

This stage is for the development of future ventures. Adults always have their own ideas and hopes. It is really important to be able to respect that those are our own expectations and passions. We must allow the child to grow his own ideas. Our role at this stage is to support whole-heartedly whatever the child presents. We can discuss it and ask how he came to that discovery? How does he feel about it? This will help him verbalise and practice communication skills. It will also let him know that the ultimate accomplishment and satisfaction is for him. He won't be performing to please the adults. If the child is able to discover every aspect of himself without shame, he will know himself. His identity. He will on his own, follow what feels good to him. This is the mission. To develop and help grow the child's own intuition without our biases.

Autonomy

In the words of Constance Kamii, "Autonomy means being governed by oneself. It is the opposite of heteronomy, which means being governed by somebody else."

It is important to encourage the child's autonomy and sense of independence. The Montessori philosophy is *teach me what I need to know so I can do it myself*. This really ought to be the motto. Allowing the child to dress himself, even though it's a lot quicker to dress him. Allowing the child to tidy up his own room, set up the table. Teaching him without correcting what he's done. Letting him self-correct. If he shows up with his shoes on the wrong way round, so what? He put them on himself. That's the important point. He will eventually realise they're not comfortable that way! He is learning and it takes time. Walking takes time, talking takes time, learning to read takes time . . . Life takes time. And that's good. Each at their own pace.

Cycles

Our role is to observe. Observe, observe, observe. An then, to set up environments that stimulate children's interests. Children are attracted to beauty. They appreciate aesthetically appealing settings. They are intrigued by cute boxes and trays and they enjoy order. Teaching them to finish cycles is really important. To finish what they start. To put things back in their place. I often hear parents complain about how children never put things away. Showing them and explaining to them the reasoning behind it helps. It's quite rare that they just "get it." We have to explain until they understand and learn. This is ultimately an important lesson for all of us. How often do we start projects when we haven't finished others yet? Having studied this for the children, I now catch myself about to go off on a tangent with a new project and I have to remind myself to finish what I started first.

Praise

Praising children is a big dilemma. On the one hand, we want to encourage them and make them feel good. On the other hand, there is our influence. Without even realising it, we might praise aspects and things that we especially value. It is so easy to do. Also, children are so sensitised to please the adults in their life. They need us for survival and they can feel our approval or not, as the case may be. They can even detect the nuances. I'm a writer, I love writing, I can't help feeling utter delight when children begin to write. For me, writing was always so soothing. I wrote diaries and journals and essays. I always felt so good after writing. So, I know that I am all about the *Literacy* part of the classroom. I feel writing is so empowering. I have to remind myself that this is my agenda. For someone else, art might be their thing. Art may have been their outlet and therefore, the environment will be very encouraging to art. There is nothing wrong with that as long as we are aware of our own biases. So I would encourage discussion over praise. "Seek first to understand before being understood" as Stephen Covey would say.

Perfect!

Let's talk about perfection. It is fine to try to perfect oneself so as to live a life of truth. There is also the educational perfecting where a child will repeat a work over and over again. This is also to perfect something deep within the child and is a necessary part of learning. However, there is a paralysing perfection that one must overcome. The need to be perfect to show up, the need to submit perfect work, the presentation of work only when it is "perfect."

The child who will need a new piece of paper and will go on and on needing new pieces of paper until the paper runs out. This attempt at perfection is utterly unnecessary. I used to suffer from this one and see it often in my classrooms, mostly in girls. So many times,

I have risked it and handed in something I felt was less than perfect and it turned out to be beautifully received. So, let's kick that need to be perfect out. Let's enable children to take risks and discover that life is messy and through the mess, we learn and grow to find our own perfection. This perfection is ours as we connect to source, to our intuition, to our inner truth. By being real and authentic, we are perfect.

Intuition

"The only real valuable thing is intuition."

Albert Einstein

*A*ristotle defined *Kairos* as the time and space in which truth becomes clear, the proof delivered! The Ancient Greeks had two words for time, *Chronos and Kairos. Chronos* is the chronological, sequential, linear concept of time. *Kairos* represents the supreme moment, the perfection of life's unfolding. *Chronos* is quantitative. *Kairos* is more qualitative in nature.

Children have no concept of time. In fact, as a concept, it's a rather complex one to teach. We sometimes create timelines so children can at least begin making sense of what comes first, followed by . . . For instance, *after school, we go home, we take a bath, we then have dinner, we go to bed, read a story and then sleep. In the morning, we wake up, we brush our teeth* and so on. Building up to seasons, holidays and so much more.

The concept of time is important because ultimately, it is the lack of it that creates so much of our chaos as adults. It's the rush to be at work on time, to make sure the kids are ready for school on time, to make sure everyone gets to sleep on time. It's almost funny, we rush to make sure we sleep enough hours so we're relaxed and feeling good the next day. Essentially, we rush to relax. I so remember my finance days when I had to be in the office at 7am because I worked with the Asian markets. Once I hit the age of thirty, my body started really needing sleep and instead of finding another job, I would rush like a maniac eating dinner, talking on the phone, getting my twenty million things done before being promptly in bed by 10pm so that I might have my eight hours sleep. Well, let me tell you, the rushing was useless, I would be wide-eyed and wired by the time I was in bed. I had done everything but unwind. There was not enough time for that!

The truth is, there is enough time for everything. For everything that is important. Everything we could possibly need in this lifetime will be ours, abundantly. Let's make the time to stop and help each other, let's remember that magical feeling of being a child where time was not of the essence. Only the caring, the gentleness, the fun, the moment mattered. Ultimately, we have no control beyond the moment. So, let's make every moment good and worthy of us.

You see ultimately, this book is about what we have to learn from children. They have been my best teachers. We all grow up so fast and then realise that it's about who we were as children. One of my best friends from Wellesley summed it up so well, "We grow up only to realise we want to recapture our core." Our core is who we are when we are born. Our most genuine authentic self. If we can hold on to that, and pursue the life our core really wants, then our purpose in this lifetime will be honourably fulfilled. By following our truth, we will prosper in every area of our life. The lessons our soul would have mapped out for us to learn, we will flow through and our life will feel enchanted.

Gentle Whisper

Deep deep within us all is a voice that is forever lovingly whispering our truth. It might be an image, a feeling, a déjà vu perception of the life we are here to experience. It is ongoing and if we pay attention, the voice becomes clearer and the vision brighter. This loving voice is our very own guidance mechanism. When we are in sync, open to ideas that guide us in that direction, we feel happy and alive. When we shut the voice and the vision down with thoughts like *it's too good to be true*, we feel sad and empty. This internal guidance is the voice of inspiration, it is empowering and life-giving and so rich with ideas and steps that gently move us towards the life of our dreams, the life our soul planned for us.

We are born deeply intuitive, very much in touch with this guidance. With time, with life, we are introduced to the rational mind. If we are paying attention, we catch it quick, the hunch emerges and instead of acting on it, we talk ourselves out of it. As simple as having an idea to call someone pop into our minds and rationalising that it's not the right time, they'll be busy, out etc. That's how intuition is over-ridden by the rational mind over and over again all day every day. The clue is that when we are acting on intuition, we feel vibrant and energetic and so in sync with life. It's miracle territory, as step by step, we move in the direction of what feels good. When life feels difficult, like we're climbing a down escalator, that is a sure sign that we have drifted away from our intuitive guidance, from the voice of inspiration. Life is supposed to be gentle and easy. When it feels like a struggle, it's time to step back, take a deep breath and ask a few questions.

Early entries on Intuition:

I've been trying to find the perfect definition for intuition. The Oxford dictionary says "immediate apprehension by the mind without reasoning, immediate insight." Hmm, I get the immediate bit but does that mean that every instinct or impulse is intuition? I don't think so . . . So many of those loud calls come from our ego, the polar opposite of intuition. And, sometimes, it's fear that directs.

It's difficult finding someone or some book or some work to fully explain intuition. Yet, intuition is what it's all about. If we can master listening to it and acting on it, our life is much easier. So intuition is a hunch, a gut feeling. Someone said "it's like an itch that won't go away." Interesting. But, ignore it long enough, and that quiet persistent voice can be pushed aside. Quite a way aside. The rational mind takes over and our heart doesn't even know it exists.

A friend of mine asked me "how do we fall in love?" He wanted to rationalise that too!

Energy is Intuition

Following our energy is following intuition. Shakti Gawain explains it so well with "When we follow our intuitive sense of what's true and right for us, and do what we genuinely feel energy for, we always seem to have enough money to be, do, and have the things we truly need and want. When we follow the flow of our energy, the universe always seems to support us financially, sometimes in very surprising and unexpected ways."

Journal entry in Paris *(early learning on following the energy, trusting it)*
   On my way to the kids' class this afternoon, I learned more about listening to intuition. I looked at my watch and knew that logically, the metro would be the quicker way there. But I looked over in the direction of the Musée d'Orsay and I felt like walking. So I walked. It was cold, very cold. I found the bus at the station. I got on and comfortably seated myself. It was the bus' terminus, so it felt like an eternity before we got started on the journey. I thought I'd get off at Concorde and metro the rest of the

way. As we arrived at Concorde, I thought I'd get out at the Champs. Again, my body didn't want to move. Even though logically, I knew that it would be quicker on the metro, there was something soothing about the view of Paris. So, I risked it, and stayed on the bus, because my energy was not moving me. I arrived at class on the dot. I followed my energy. The mind would have had me move but my body didn't want to.

That's a good lesson for me . . . I sat there not knowing if it would work out. All I knew was that I was happy on the bus! It sounds so simple but how often do we move ourselves out of fear? Our intuition knows what it's doing, always. What's sometimes hard is to separate the ego's voice from that of intuition. What I'm learning is that intuition is not necessarily the first voice. The ego offers the voice of fear. When the heart talks, it's out of appeal. That option calls to you, it has the energy with it. It's not the one that feels like a "should."

At first, it feels a little scary. We're vulnerable to not knowing for sure. We just know that we're comfortable in the now. I guess that's all we need really.

In Sync

Children are such a source of love. They unite us all. Everyone, no matter what nationality, race, religion will lighten up in the presence of a child. Dr Maria Montessori believed it is through children that we may strive for a united world. Children are love. They are pure love. They take in their environment and they love everything about it. Children are naturally drawn to nature and to beauty. Children are loving no matter what. They are happy joyful beings open and ready to discover the world.

A lifetime is then spent in search of what feels good. We are all looking to find that state of inner joy and peace. Yet this is how we come into the world. As adults, we can interfere not only by making children feel insecure but by breaking their will. It is so easy to do that. But why would we want to? Sure they will obey us. They have no choice. They need us to survive, but it is really us who will find in them our salvation. Would we therefore not prefer to obey them?

I remember one beautiful summer day a few years ago in New York City. I was with my three and a half year old niece. We were heading to Central Park. After a subway ride uptown, and a few blocks of walking, she said she was hungry. We had just finished breakfast, and we were almost at the park. I tried to convince her to continue on to the park by promoting all the fun awaiting us there. I was thinking, she'll play and move around a little, and then we'll stop for a good lunch. She insisted that she was starving and had to eat immediately. So, we stopped in a little cafe and ordered. Lo and behold, we looked out of the window and the sky was black. It started raining so violently I couldn't believe it. This might have happened whilst we were in the middle of the park with all our bits and pieces. Well, we ate, talked, laughed and by the time we were paying the bill, the sun was shining again! It felt so enchanted. Children are like that. They are naturally in sync. When we follow them, we join that enchanted path.

Enchanted Path

We are all born with a mission, a higher purpose. The more we are following our intuition, the sooner we will realise it. We are each unique and with our very own contribution to make. Our mere existence is a gift into the universe. If we follow our truth and are always heading in the direction that feels good to our soul, our life is easy. Complications arise when we are not being true to ourselves. We are somehow resisting our natural path. Life is not meant to be difficult. When we are guided by our higher purpose, our inner guidance will show us the way. We will always be in the right place at the right time. A friend of mine once told me "Do what you love." It's as simple as that.

For adults, the way to connect with our intuition is by quietening the mind. This happens naturally when we are close to nature. Nature shows us that every part that exists in plant, flower and animal is within us too. Another way is to breathe deeply. Just breathe. Meditation is basically a series of deep breaths. We focus on the breath in and out and let the thoughts fall away. In such peaceful states, we are able to connect to our core. We feel energised and clear again. Just fifteen minutes a day where we let the brain rest from all the thoughts is enough to bring us back in touch with our truth, our naturally joyful state.

Right/Left Brain

Research suggests that we are using under ten percent of our brain's capacity. So, what's the other ninety percent up to? Let's consider that we have two parts to the brain, the right side and the left side. The right brain takes in the spatial and the artistic. The right brain sees in images. It is our creative side. It is holistic and intuitive. Our left brain is more linear in reasoning. Logic and mathematics come from the left side of our brain. Our left brain is analytic and verbal. In order for our left brain to go out into the world and use its more logical and verbal skills, it needs ideas. Ideas come from the right side. So really, what we are looking to do is listen to the intuition from the right brain and take action with the left.

In Western society, we have focused on the left side of the brain at the expense of the right. We encourage children to be logical. Schools rate verbal and mathematical skills above all else. Anything stemming from the right side of the brain is relegated to emotional—unknown, and therefore scary! In the

East, a lot more emphasis is placed on the more holistic, intuitive side. The rhythm of life, spatial arts and yoga all encourage more introspection and understanding of self. However, action was not the focus. Until now.

What's encouraging is that the big nations in the West and the East are beginning to explore and learn from each other. They are starting to incorporate the theories from 'the other side.' We see yoga and martial arts growing in the West. And we see the more proactive mentality appearing in the East with some of the most dynamic businesses now emerging from there. In the West, we are asking "what are we feeling?" and in the East, the question is "what shall we do about it?"

The idea for the West is to have a chance to quieten the more logical rational mind in order to become in touch with the core we were born with. Essentially, to unlearn what society and the education system have taught us! To become more in touch with who we really are so we can eventually do what we are here to do and excel at it—easily. Better health, more happiness and a rising energy are the byproducts of that. Just look at children—notice their energy, their enthusiasm for life. Ulcers, migraines, depression are all results of too much brain logic. When we are listening to our intuition and acting on it, our life makes total sense.

We know when something feels off. We know it in our gut. And when we ignore it long enough, our body takes action by reflecting our dis-ease to us. Accidents often happen to cause us to stop and review. It is always worth remembering that our trials—all the difficulties we encounter in life—stem from a lesson our soul is itching for us to learn.

Imagination

So many of us operate mainly using our left brain, the logical verbal part. Our right brain is the visual, more intuitive and creative part of our brain. By choosing to tap into the right brain, we activate the imagination. As children, there is usually a lot of imagination at play.

Through visualising, we can actually begin the process of bringing about our desires and our goals. Top athletes visualise their games before actually going out there to perform the win. Thoughts lead to action. An artist first imagines his work and then creates it.

Children do this naturally. They spend so much time in their imagination. As models, we take them into the left side of their brain with all the logic. Intuition comes from the right. It is so easy to contradict it with logic. We really want to encourage children's imagination. By imagining first, we let the idea direct us to the action.

Step by Step

I have a friend whose daughter has been waking up in the middle of the night recently and nothing seemed to be helping. As I was writing about *attachment* for this book, I suddenly had an idea that this friend's daughter was not feeling securely attached. I was preparing a cup of tea and had the idea to call her. I looked at the time and thought, this is not the best time to reach her. But I still felt like calling, so I ignored the rational and called. I offered my thoughts and she was in awe of my timing. She said that she was just contemplating ideas for her daughter and really needed to hear this. She sent me a message a few hours later thanking me for my call and said that everything I said was spot on.

At the risk of offending my friend by telling her that her daughter was insecurely attached, and at the risk of calling at the *wrong* time, this turned out to be a very important phone call. Not only for my friend and her relationship with her daughter, but also for me. It was yet another lesson in following intuition just as I was writing about it for this book. Also, every once in a while, I would wonder who was I to be writing this book. This phone call gave me the courage to continue, knowing that I had something important to share.

This is how intuition guides us. I ended up glued to my computer the entire rest of the day, motivated to get my ideas out there asap!

This is when we start to feel the synchronicity, as people and events line up to lead us to our goal. It is revolutionary.

Silence

"To the mind that is still,
the whole universe surrenders"

Lao Tse

*T*he Beatles had entire songs dictated to them in meditation. Michelangelo saw the angel in the marble and carved around it. Einstein had his best ideas in the midst of nature walks!

Our Magnificent Life

Since we were children, we have been imagining bits and pieces of our life. We have a vision of what our dream life looks like. This vision has been in the making our entire life. Some would argue even before conception—A soul plan. This vision keeps popping up as our perfect life. We have flashes and déjà-vus and certain sentences or conversations that most resonate with our deepest being. Sometimes, we quieten it down by thinking it's too good to be true. But that vision perseveres and continues to come up intermittently. It takes us with it for a moment every time . . . Like this long distant dream. If we're lucky, very lucky, at one point in our life, we resurrect it. And begin to construct it, one piece at a time.

This vision is our soul's plan for us because when we are focusing on it, thinking about it, dreaming it up, we are so alive and happy. We can feel our inner flame vibrant and powerful. That vision is the way. It is the road, it is the path, it is the journey and it is the destination. This is the life we are here to live.

The vision is very unique to each one of us, it is tailor-made for us. It incorporates all that we love, what we are naturally good at, and the elements of our life that mesh together to come up with the whole. We wouldn't be able to imagine it, if it wasn't ours. And it wouldn't feel so perfect and rich and satisfying just thinking about it. It takes us into a world that feels good and right, a place where we are powerful. This is where we co-create, with Source energy, the life our deepest being knows is ours.

Yin and Yang

We all have two kinds of energies within us. The feminine energy of *being*. This a more receptive and open energy. It is intuitive, nurturing and calm. And the masculine energy of *doing*. This is a more action-orientated type of energy. This is the more logical, rational energy.

The Chinese talk of *Yin* and *Yang* as opposing forces, interconnected and interdependent. *Yin* is female, receptive, yielding. *Yang* is male, active, initiating. Like an undertow in the ocean, every advance is complemented by a retreat. We must keep this in mind when appreciating characteristics. We need both to be complete.

In stillness, we know ourselves. Through being authentic, meditating, reflecting, imagining and praying, the *yin* is accessed. Then, the *yang* energy comes in and follows through with the action. This is the energy that gets things done, that takes intuitive ideas and makes them happen. The seed is planted first and then it grows into a beautiful plant. And so must our life. The more fertile and rich the soil, the healthier and more beautiful the plant. So take the time to work on your soil. It is through our most profound truth that our soul speaks to us.

Mother Nature

Nature is the best connector to the intuitive, receptive, *yin* energy. Nature allows us to go deep within. In nature is our own nature. Everything in nature is within ourselves. The steadiness of the trunk of the tree, the leaves that change colours and textures with the seasons, the birds that fly and sing, the flowers that blossom and bloom.

We follow nature's rhythms. The best time to create is always Spring. We make our creation materialise in the Summer. We start a more inward journey in the Autumn and Winter, preparing to create again for the Spring. Our energy is at its highest with the warmth of the sun.

Nature is the best way to switch off the noise of the city. Whether it's a park or the countryside or the mountains and the sea, we need time in nature. We need to balance the action energy by being in nature's gentleness.

Children and nature have a special affinity. Have you ever noticed how after a five minute walk in the city, the child will complain of being exhausted? Whereas, the same child can walk and wander around in nature for hours on end.

Nature is magical, and not just for children. We are all in closer touch with our souls out in nature. Nature reminds us of life's simplicity and its natural beauty. Everything we need is within us and nature fills us with that love and nurturance.

When we teach children about nature. The cycle of things. How a seed grows. How a caterpillar becomes a butterfly. Children will always be in sync with nature. Children who understand about plants and flowers are not likely to pick them but rather to savour their beauty. Children love to look after plants and animals, watering and feeding as necessary. They will observe with fascination the growth and development. They will naturally appreciate nature.

Children cooped up indoors become quite rowdy and impatient sometimes. The moment we take them out into nature, these same children are peaceful and serene as they go about their discoveries. So nature offers food for the soul, natural movement for the body, mental stimulation, the understanding of the interconnectedness of life, peace of mind and fresh air!

It is so important to allow children to explore nature, to commune with nature, to feel the freedom of nature, as they run barefoot on the grass and stretch their bodies. This, for children, is life.

We used to do a study of Trees in the classroom. We would look around, and figure out what comes from trees: the chairs, the tables, the pencils, the paper, the doors, the cupboards, the cutting boards, the apples, the nuts, the maple syrup, the air we breathe. Trees also hold bird nests and cocoons. So much animal life depends on trees. And then, we would start a *Recycling* programme. As children become more aware of the importance of trees in our lives, they become interested in their preservation. They would look for materials in the recycling bin first. The paper, barely used before, would now be back in action! This stays with children forever as they grow and contribute to the environment.

Mother Nature needs us all and we need her. Children need to feel her freedom and her strength and realise that this is also within them. As they grow and create their lives, nature will be such a healthy source of comfort to them.

The Pyramid

In her beautiful work on *Creative Visualization*, Shakti Gawain discusses the triangle of *Being, Doing and*

Having. Most of us begin the other way around . . . We believe that by *having*, we will be in a position of *doing* what we like and as a result, *being* who we want to be. But no amount of *having* can actually offer that peace of mind. It becomes a spiral—the more we have, the more we need. So, in fact, we move further and further away from our true essence. Sometimes, we'll have visions of our dream life by the sea or those lavender fields. Deep within, our soul will feel good just thinking about it. But we'll go back to the logic of things and the ego mind will convince us that we can't take that kind of risk. The ego will tell us to continue along that dreadful route of earning and spending and dreaming. What is a life without risk? And what is the risk of listening to our heart after all? What risk is there in knowing who we are and living a life that makes sense to our truth? Essentially, a life of *being, doing and having* what we love.

I once read a story about a man who lived near the sea. He would go out everyday and fish. By evening, he would come home and eat a healthy seafood dinner with his loved ones, enjoying the sunset and the warmth of family. He would sell his fish at the market where he savoured loyal clients' appreciation.

One day, a business school graduate visits the village. He notices the incredible selection of fish this man is able to procure daily. He talks to him about developing this business into a *real* business which can grow and multiply and eventually even list on the stock exchange.

He talks to the man of the potential wealth that he and his family can aspire to. He explains that the man may need to relocate to the city to oversee the growth of the business and that he would need to travel to promote the brand.

This, of course, would imply spending a lot less time with the family and a generally more hectic lifestyle. When the fisherman expresses concern, the man replies, "But when you retire, you will be able to live a more peaceful life by the sea in a cute village and spend more quality time with your family and loved ones."

We live our lives backwards, don't we?!

So, actually, the pyramid is *Being* who we are, *Doing* what we love, and *Having* what we need to live our perfect life.

The Answer is in the Silence

Much has been written about the benefits of meditation. It has been used successfully to cure illnesses that were deemed incurable. It is, in fact, now being introduced in some of the most important businesses as a tool to help us tap into our deepest creativity. Carl Jung discussed the collective unconscious. Meditation is the road to accessing this other world so rich in information.

I love this definition: *Prayer is the question and meditation the answer.* It makes total sense. How might we possibly reach deep within to understand anything in the hustle and bustle of day to day life? The answer might be staring us in the face and chances are, we'd miss it. Like hamsters going round and round in circles, over and over again . . .

It's time to stop, to breathe, and to listen!

Meditation 101

Sit comfortably, legs crossed, back straight and close your eyes. Make sure you are somewhere where you will not be disturbed. Switch off phones (or silent!). Take a deep breath. Follow your breath in and out. Thoughts might pop in. No worries. Just let them go with the breath. Imagine relaxing your body starting with your head, then your shoulders, then your stomach, then your legs and eventually your toes. You can go as slowly and as detailed as you like on the parts of the body that you are relaxing. At each juncture, relax into a deep breath, as in silently say or think "My back is relaxed" and take a deep breath into the back. When you have reached your toes and relaxed them with a good breath, silently count from ten to zero backwards. All the time, thoughts might try to barge in to your mind. That's okay, just keep going with your countdown and breathing. Then, imagine white light coming through your head. Linger for a moment with the light at your *third eye*, the point on your forehead just above and between the eyes. This is your centre of Intuition, also called the *mind's eye*. Then, move the light from there into your heart. Imagine your heart glowing with this light. Now ask your heart any question you have . . . And wait. The answer will come either right there and then, or later through a phone call with a friend or a sign on the bus the next day! You will have your answer.

Use this technique for any question you may have. The answer is coming from your deepest truth, the part of you that is connected to Source energy. The part of you that is Love.

This is really worth doing before big decisions. You will begin trusting this process so much that checking in with your inner guidance will become second nature on every subject. When we act from that place, we never regret, ponder or dwell on our actions. They feel guided and correct. A very peaceful place from which we reach higher and higher.

The Silence Game

Dr. Maria Montessori introduced the *Silence Game* in classrooms. As a lot of us know, once children have learned to speak, nothing will make them stop. They are so full of questions and discoveries. We want to encourage that. The *Silence Game* is an exercise in self-control. It is extremely hard for a child to be silent. Compare it to our minds that are constantly chattering. For children, it's happening on the outside! When we try to meditate, we are in fact attempting to quiet the mind, giving it a chance to find its essence again. When children practice the *Silence Game*, they are attempting to control their own chattering. When a child succeeds, he is filled with pride and satisfaction. And they glow afterwards.

Freedom

A Course in Miracles teaches that "in your freedom lies the freedom of the world." Many of us have known controlling environments. With all good intentions, decisions were taken on our behalf. Often, we invite that dynamic again in relationships or our work life. It's familiar territory. It takes having a rough experience or an epiphany of some sort to help us break that pattern. And, sometimes, life decides for us that *Enough is Enough!*

Freedom is the name of the game. We are here to be happy and freedom is a major road in that direction. Choosing what we love, doing what we love, pursuing what we love. It all comes down to us. It takes bold courage to be free. Totally free. Free from what others think. Free to self-express as we like. When we don't, something feels off. We feel like there is someone else inside of us and we are holding that free spirit prisoner.

Whatever scares us is very often the exact right next step for us. It's our soul itching to grow, to expand. We are here to feel that freedom in the same way all God's creations in nature live and blossom.

So, next time the energy moves you to do something, allow yourself to do it. Notice the resistance come up. Know that this is completely normal. Now tell yourself, *I really don't have to do it afterall* . . . And let the inspiration lead you there willingly. As Rumi wrote, "Let yourself be silently drawn by the stronger pull of what you really love."

Words

"I believe that unarmed truth and unconditional love will have the final word in reality."

Martin Luther King, Jr.

*C*ontrary to what is sometimes thought to be best for the child, leaving him in peace isolated in his room and sleeping as much as possible is actually detrimental to his mental hunger and eventually, to his overall development. He is not ill after all, he is born.

In an ideal world, one would keep the baby close for as long as possible. In being physically close, one is assuring his healthy attachment whilst opening an array of images through the adult's life. In observation of such a way of life, where the child is carried close with his eyes looking out into the world, whilst the adult is conducting the activities of the day, the child never cries. He may fall asleep but unless ill or hurt, he will not cry. He is satisfied and can continue his happy discovery of this world. He is also accessing words, which will eventually contribute to his solid grasp of language.

By six months, the child can live without his mother's milk, his first tooth appears and he begins to utter his first syllables. He is therefore already en route to independence. This is a big milestone for not only is his mobility beginning so is his attempt at language. Whilst some adults repeat the monosyllabic first syllables back at a child, what a child actually needs is to hear words. Full-fledged words. This is how he learns to speak, by hearing language. The child's natural quest for independence is a big motivator for language and as such, communication. The child will be able to clearly express his needs and will no longer be dependent on the adult guessing for him.

Delta waves at birth

In his fascinating book *The Biology of Belief*, Bruce H. Lipton, PhD., examines the science by which cells receive and process information. It turns out "DNA is controlled by signals from *outside* the cell, including the energetic messages emanating from our positive and negative thoughts."

Here we are trying to meditate and relax into calmer delta waves as adults. It turns out that from birth to two years old, this is our natural brain wave, hence how open we are to absorbing our environment. Dr. Maria Montessori, the first woman to graduate from medical school in Italy in 1896, discussed the child's absorbent mind in all her work. Now scientists are confirming the EEC frequency of the brain at different ages.

From a parenting point of view, this is important because later on in adulthood, when we are revisiting our belief systems, we are having to practically reprogramme ourselves into a state of acceptance of the new. However, in childhood, we are wide open to take it in the way those around us see it. So, to avoid much hard work later, how about we start children off on the right note? Everything is possible. The glass is half full, it's our choice after all.

According to Dr. Rima Laibow in *Quantitative EEG and Neurofeedback*, children between the age of two and six move up to a higher level of EEG activity, theta (4-8 Hz). Theta brain wave is when our subconscious is most open to downloading information. For very advanced hypnosis! Essentially, whatever the children are hearing at around that age, will be embedded in their subconscious. This information will guide them throughout their lives. So, you decide, "Stupid child" or "You can do anything!"

The Hand and the Brain

Intelligence begins with the hand. The baby initially feels the world through his senses. He touches to know, to discover and to understand. Maria Montessori said never give the brain more than the hand can handle. A child learns to walk using his hands, learns to talk using his hands, learns to write using his hands. The child masters movements with his hands. Everyone walks the same in the end but no one knows what a person's hand is capable of.

Drama

The toddler is now attempting language on top of walking. Whilst the child is trying to express himself, he really needs to know that you are trying to understand him. Utter frustration at not being understood, coupled with a huge sensitivity during this period, often cause what we perceive as tantrums. If the child knows that you are on his side, going around with him trying to figure it out, there will not be this utter frustration on his side. It is this misunderstanding that causes so much grief for both adults and children at this stage.

Two things also worth noting here. One is the child's fascination and need for order, and the other is the child's patience. If you are unable to understand a message, look into the possibility that it might have to do with putting something back in its place, or something the child has been waiting for from earlier on that day. So, remember, you are the child's "interpreter." You are on the same side. Let him be sure of that fact.

Biting

Children who are frustrated by lack of words often bite as a communication method. Be their "interpreter." Help them with the words and with making sense of the emotion. We have to learn conflict management through adults who teach us the words and the way. When I see something brewing—Hands getting ready and an emotion building, it is usually enough for me to say "Use your words" for the child to pull back and realise that there is another way. No one enjoys conflict. We are all looking to be understood. Help the child. Be there for him. We are his example. The way we deal with difficult situations is the way he will learn to respond going forward.

Language

Children learn vocabulary through exposure. A French mother was learning Mandarin for a business assignment coming up. She was constantly playing audio CDs at home and repeating the words and sentences. Her three year old, in the background, picked it up faster than her! Unconsciously.

People are fascinated by how from one day to the next, a child suddenly begins speaking a language, correct accent and all. Children learn languages by hearing them. Their brains are wired to take in the words that are often repeated. Opportunities to present vocabulary can be maximised in the most natural settings. Unloading the groceries, preparing dinner, setting up the table, going to the bank . . . Parents, teachers, caregivers, grandparents, godparents, babysitters: Please talk, talk, talk! Pronouncing the words clearly, pointing to objects, helping to associate print to actual things.

Bilingualism

One parent speaks one language and the other, the second language. Being consistent is very important. Even if the child addresses you in the more dominant language, continue the exposure to your language. Reading, writing, movies, everything in your language.

Trilingualism

School or the grandmother or the caregiver is the third language exposure. The key is consistency, so the child is clear on who speaks what. There will always be a more dominant language. It usually tends to be the language of the country where the child lives. Since language acquisition in childhood is about exposure, whichever language is most accessed, will become the dominant one.

Children will often mix up the languages. Sentences might include words from each language. Without correcting, we just rephrase it fully in one language according to our language association. So if we are the French speaking parent, we would rephrase it entirely in French. Not to correct, just so the child hears the new words and structure. It's all about exposure. And their brains will eventually separate the languages out. In the meantime, enjoy the Franglais!

Language is so much more than words. Art is language. Music is language, Movement is language. If we remember that we are greeting a soul into the world.

A soul who comes equipped with a lot more than we think! The more authentic we are ourselves, the more in sync we will be with the child. If we are living a life of truth ourselves, then this will be the core of the child's primary relationship. All that we can be sure of is that in being open-hearted and loving, we will tune in to the child's needs and this is the beginning of language.

Language is our primary method of communication. It is by no means the only one but it is a direct way to ask for what we need. If we tune in to the child, soul to soul, then language is only an accompaniment for all sorts of other communication. Sometimes, we know telepathically what someone needs. Still, language is essential. Language is for expressing oneself, orally and in writing.

Music

Confucius said "Music creates a kind of pleasure which human nature cannot do without." Songs and music are another good language introduction. Children love music. They can learn songs in languages they don't even understand purely for the pleasure of it. What a lovely way to expose children to different cultures and melodies. So sing away, play music for them while they are preparing themselves. And in the car, and whilst cooking. Animate their life with music, it's magical. Plus, it's easy language exposure.

Films

Even I sometimes have to resort to that Aristocats DVD! There are times when we really have to do something and we know that TV is going to help us out. Children are mesmerised in front of TV. They're gonners once that Dora programme begins. The thing is we don't want to lose interaction possibilities. So, my advice is watch their reactions, ask them about what they have watched. What did they enjoy about it? What scared them? What made them laugh? Films and TV programmes are sometimes a great second language exposure. Most children's DVDs these days offer language options, so we can also extract a bonus out of the experience.

The point is to just not lose them in front of the TV, more of an accompaniment to creative outlets. Let them draw things or write stories or build with blocks or have dramatic play moments. Children need to use their imagination. We all do.

Whenever we teach children to creatively visualise what they want, they jump at the concept. Yet, children do this naturally with anything they can get their hands on. Don't feel you need to buy them costumes and gears, children imagine with anything. Nature is a particularly wonderful dwelling.

Story Telling ══════════════════════════════

Ask children to tell you stories and be prepared to listen. Help them along with "Mm" "and then" and let them get to the end of their story. Really listen. They might be letting you in on something that is on their mind, even something that is troubling them. Children learn about emotions and how to express them through us. We help them attain the necessary vocabulary for what they are trying to share. Help them re-phrase sentences correctly, add vocabulary if necessary. The key is to make sure you are truly listening to their essence. Enrich their styles by words, not substance. It is their message, their story. They just need us to guide them along, not to create for them.

Dramatic play is very important for expressive language. Children exercise different tones through these make believe scenes. You can also see yourself in their dramatic play. When they are pretending to be the parent or the teacher or the caregiver or the grandmother, you can see what you've been modelling. Do you bark orders at them, do you remember to say please and thank you? It's hugely revealing, and sometimes a bit of a wake-up call. Remember children model us. Not what we tell them, but how we tell them. Not advice on their behaviour but our own behaviour. It's very telling.

Story telling is, in fact, the very beginning of literacy. This can be elaborated on in print, through drawings, scribbles and invented writing. We can encourage the child by complimenting him on a great story and suggesting we find a way to keep that story. "Why don't you write it down so we can read it again later?" This is also a technique you can use if you really don't have the time to listen to a full story at that moment. By suggesting that the child puts it down on paper, he understands that you do care to hear about it, just that you can't right at that moment. His eagerness to capture the details may even motivate him further to produce a wonderfully satisfying story. Make sure you do make the time, at some point, to listen to it. Perhaps at night, as a bedtime story. This is how Beatrix Potter got started. She would tell her own stories at bedtime!

Writing

The writing may be scribbles to begin with, or it may be drawings. It may be both. The writing will eventually start to look more and more like letters and eventually the child will make up spellings based on sounds until they lead to the word itself. On this note, it is important to mention the concept of sounds. Sometimes, adults are really keen to teach letters to children—the alphabet. One important advice is teach the sound of the letter more than its name as this is what children tap into when they begin constructing words. This is also quite a fun game to play when you are en route somewhere or in the supermarket queue and so on. "Mmmm" Mia, mmm mother, mmm meow, mmm monkey, mmm mushroom.

There are lots of language games one can play like that. The rhyming game: "bat, cat, fat, mat, rat, sat . . . ." Children so enjoy these games. Plus, they're educational and they help with their language abilities. There are cards one can buy to assist with play. Or, like we did in Montessori schools, creating our own cards and even laminating them so they last longer.

Scribbles are the beginning of writing and must be encouraged. Involve children in what you are doing. Montessori discovered that children prefer real work to play. Let them feel useful. Ask them to help you with the list of what you need to buy at the market. Let them write the list. They can draw or scribble. Ask them to write you notes to remind you of things that need to get done. Pretend you have too much to do and let the child feel helpful in making notes and lists and recipes for you. Ask a child to read it to you. His story, his list, his request has a lot more to say than what you see in those scribbles!

As you go about running errands, use the opportunity to point print to children, so they realise its uses. Street names, marked items, instructions. When you read, point your finger to words. Trace the sentences, so they conceptualise where the sentence begins and ends i.e. From left to right in French and English, from right to left in Arabic and Hebrew.

This meshes straight into *Reading*. A child's reading flows from writing. Letter sounds, first sounds, last sounds, beginning of sentences, end of sentences, paragraphs, punctuation. How the voice goes up if there's an exclamation mark at the end of the sentence. Children love that! Dr. Montessori's *Language* materials are wonderful. Children truly enjoy them and they are the ultimate in brain memory. The hand teaches the brain. Two favourites for language are *Sandpaper Letters* to teach children to trace the letters and associate with the sound and the *Moveable Alphabet* which allows the beginning of word creation for reading and writing.

Reading

Since it's all about exposure, reading is vital. All sorts of books. The more interactive books are great for the initial attention grasp of the very little ones. Books where children can touch different textures, hear different sounds, see themselves in mirrors reflecting back. Reading is also a bonding time with the adult. The child is snuggled up, usually in the arms of, there is touch and warmth and a feeling of closeness. This way, reading and its exposure are associated with something highly enjoyable. This is the child's first experience with print and its connection to language. Each picture has words that go along with it. Pictures tell a story. Pronounce the words, looking at the child, watching the reactions. Discover what makes him laugh and feel good, see what captures him, and encourage more of that subject.

Children are usually very interested in books that mean something to them. Elaborating on those subjects is great. Sometimes, the child will want to read the same book over and over and over again. There is something in that book that is calling out to him. Sometimes, it's just that the book is tackling something he wants to figure out: sleeping in the dark, potty training, school.

The child needs to hear words in order to learn words. We have to be talkative, even if it is a little forced at first. Children's neurons are wired to register the words that are most often repeated. Remember that you are doing them a favour and helping in their development. By explaining things and being available, you are contributing to their sense of importance in the world. They are learning to self-regulate through your explanations. You are helping in their language performance at school. You are helping them communicate. Ultimately, so much of life—personally and professionally—is based on good communication. The child is counting on you for that exposure. If you have multiple languages at home, make the best of that situation by offering the child those possibilities for the future.

The Power of Words

Mahatma Gandhi expresses it perfectly:

Your beliefs become your thoughts
Your thoughts become your words
Your words become your actions
Your actions become your habits
Your habits become your values
Your values become your destiny

A belief is a thought we keep thinking, as Abraham Hicks so ingeniously reminds us! Our thoughts become our words. The words lead to our behaviour, and *that* essentially determines our life.

We are therefore responsible for that sequence. If we hold certain beliefs that feel limiting, we have the option of changing them. The mind is very powerful. It is up to us to feed it what would serve our big picture ideas. The thoughts we allow our mind to entertain are entirely our choice. Granted, it takes some work to observe the thoughts and notice the fearful ones. The easiest way to know if a thought is moving us in the right direction, is simply by the way we feel. Expansive thoughts make us feel good, powerful, free. Limiting thoughts cause us to clam up. We literally tighten up physically.

When we have a thought that feels fearful to our whole being and we expand on it with words, our entire body reacts. It takes on a life of its own. This is where breathing comes in. Both movement and meditation transform those thoughts. Movement empowers us physically, as it shifts the fear out of the body. Meditation allows us to open up to a new perspective. Being in the present always brings us back to our point of power. From here, ideas pop up. Essentially, our intuition begins to deliver the messages that will move us along in the right direction.

This is a universe of infinite possibilities. When we open our consciousness to miracles, we receive them. Again, that happens at the belief level, which brings up the matching thoughts and leads to the words we speak. A simple statement like "I believe in miracles" is brimming with power. What we believe manifests. And it really is a matter of *faking it until you make it.*

The subconscious is the part of our mind that creates our experience. Albert Einstein observed that "the true sign of intelligence is not knowledge but imagination." Psychologists confirm that the subconscious doesn't distinguish between imagination and reality. What we say is subconsciously recorded and acted upon. If you tell yourself that you are strong, you become *strong.* It is muscle memory, the more we practice saying powerful statements, the more our subconscious goes into action to deliver on those messages.

Think of the Oscar winners who recount how they practiced their speeches as teenagers in front of the mirror, as they brushed their teeth. The toothpaste becoming the award!

Just like when we are looking for something and we absolutely cannot find it. We move on and do something else, and at another moment, we remember where that item is. The subconscious continued working on it, even though we'd moved on to something else.

So, even if we don't believe the words at first, saying and repeating them is a very powerful exercise. Reminders of the messages posted everywhere, from the fridge to the mirror are good too. While brushing our teeth, we practice. Before leaving the house, we remember. It becomes a bit funny in the end, and some of the words grow into songs and dances. The point is that this is very powerful messaging for the subconscious. Even if our logical brain resists at first, eventually, we hit a tipping point and life begins to deliver on those messages.

When I was in Paris, I would constantly chime that I was *divinely irresistible* to my soulmate. And as life would have it . . . When I moved to London and met my new *assignment*, he kept saying that I was just "irresistible." Being a lawyer and therefore very precise with his words, the *irresistible* factor clearly resonated!

Energy

"Don't ask what the world needs.
Ask what makes you come alive, and then go do it.
Because what the world needs is
people who have come alive."

Howard Thurman

*I*nspired: in-spirit means ensuring that our inner flame is shining brightly. What brings your spirit to life? We know that feeling when our eyes are twinkling and our hearts are smiling. Moments when we feel so inspired and empowered, ideas flow through us and we are so eager and willing to go with them. The more we allow our spirit to shine by moving in that direction, the more inspired and inspiring is our life.

What do you love love love? Music, dancing, flowers, delicious everything, good conversation, kissing, laughing, sunsets, gentleness . . . Make a list, a free-flowing list of everything that makes your heart sing and often, very often, think of these things. If a thought makes you happy, you know you're on the right track!

The idea is, a little more and More and MORE of what you love and LESS, Less, less of what you don't—daily. As simple as adding a walk a day might change your life (remember Einstein had his best ideas in the the midst of those!) Connecting with our spirit is our way of connecting to Source energy. Creativity stems from that place.

As we tap into what truly fascinates us, our life begins. The energy we derive from pursuing these natural interests keeps us open to more. Ideas build up and eventually, we piece it together—Our deepest truth. And from that truth, emerges our most inspired life.

Thomas Edison said "I never did a day's work in my life. It was all fun." And this, after "I have not failed. I found 10,000 ways that won't work." The point is that the journey was fun. When we are pursuing something that comes from our deepest inspiration, we have will-power and perseverance. Our spirit just won't take no for an answer. Every obstacle becomes a challenge. We are growing in the process and becoming our best.

One small step everyday in the direction of what feels good is the recipe. Even google-searching something you love is a start. One action a day leads to another, and another. And somehow, the universe joins in to support that energy by opening the right doors. Helpful people begin to show up. It's the concept of when the student is ready, the teacher appears.

Carpe diem!

There is a feeling we are after. Whatever it is that we want, it is because we believe that when we have it, we will feel a certain way. Happy. Confident. Safe. Beautiful. Powerful. Wealthy. Free. And much more. Mostly, it's a combination of feelings we're after. For instance, I want to feel inspired, divinely irresistible and peaceful. And I want it to be easy and fun and abundant!

We have to capture the feelings we're after now. Music inspires me, passionate people enchant me and Mother Nature makes me feel peaceful. So I know how to tune in to my desired feelings now. When I am in those states that feel so good to my soul, I am a magnet for everything that I want. I'm on the same wavelength as my desires. Ideas flow through me and I tend to be in the right place at the right time. It's easy, it's fun and it's abundant!

Imagine that we want to listen to Jazz on the radio, we have to find the right frequency and we will be exposed to the best Jazz on Jazz FM, for instance. If we're not on the right frequency, we'll get some other tunes . . . So that's the key, we must be on the same vibe as our desires in order for them to manifest. Misery attracts misery. It's complicated, choppy and very unsatisfying because we know that our spirit is capable of so much more. We are very powerful and when we understand this vibration business, we are on a roll. It's rock & roll to everything that our heart desires.

Find the Feeling

Take a moment to sit in silence. Close your eyes and try to remember a time when you felt the desired feelings. If no memory comes up, imagine the feeling. Go there vividly with images, sounds, scents, textures, colours. Make it very vibrant and bring it close-up. 3D! Hang in there for a bit and when you have captured the feeling, bring your thumb and any other finger together and accompany this with a statement: "I am Wealthy" or "I am Confident." Repeat this for all your desired feelings. And anytime you need to conjure up the feelings, just do the manual thumb touch and you will be there.

Remember, the universe responds to feelings. It doesn't distinguish between past, present and future. It just responds to feelings. So the more you hang out in your desired feelings, the quicker the manifestation. This is more important than all the legwork you will ever do. Essentially, from that space, the best ideas will emerge. And acting on those will prove to be a far more efficient way of achieving the goals.

Do whatever it takes to capture the feelings. Imagine, self-soothe, dance, watch the sunset, play with a child . . . Whatever takes you there!

How do you Self-Soothe?

Remember when you were a kid—How did you recalibrate after drama? After a crying fit for instance . . . Children left to their own devices will enter another world. A world of their making—imaginary friends, cars, scenarios, songs, dance. And within minutes, they have self-soothed and their vibration has completely been changed to one of joy or peace. That, is magic. They choose, maybe subconsciously at this stage, a way into a better feeling.

We adults have that option too. A bubble bath, a walk in nature, calling someone who makes us laugh, a good book, a swim, cooking, gardening, dancing. So many ways to move into a better feeling.

Note that these self-soothing options don't involve alcohol, sweets or other destructive and very short-term band-aid solutions.

We have to know how to shift vibration. *That* is essentially one of the biggest secrets to manifesting miracles.

Remember, to receive our good, we have to vibrate at the same frequency. Like attracts like. In misery, we cannot possibly attract our good. Part of the manifestation involves shifting into a better feeling. From there, the work is done. Just hanging out in that space. Essentially making happiness a full-time job. And then, just watching the manifestations join us, one by one.

As *A Course in Miracles* says, "The miracle is therefore a lesson in what joy is."

Procrastination

Deep deep within us, we have an idea of how we'd like to spend our days. We know the rhythm we enjoy. We know what we would do all day. Think of how you procrastinate when you have something that must be done. That procrastination tells a lot about what you really like. It's what we would do for free and what we do for pleasure that encompasses the work we are really here for. That's the life we are here to live. Being excited to wake up in the morning. No difference between Monday or Saturday—Lit up and passionate to do more, discover more, contribute more.

Whether we get that thrill from being a Mum or a great cook or a super gardener or by being Gordon Gekko, doesn't really matter. Our thrill usually includes both our passion and what we're naturally good at. Think of the charities you support or the causes that touch you. And what are you really good at? As in, time flies and the result is amazing, especially to you. What do you love to create: Photo albums, music playlists, chocolate chip cookies, divine book shelves . . . What do people ask you for? What makes you feel hugely useful? All these are components of the work we came here to do.

Essentially, there are no mistakes. So whatever work we have done up until today is actually going to feature in one way or another in our purpose. Our ultimate work, the work we are born to do, is a combination of all that we are good at and all that we love, coupled with our life experience and what makes us smile!

What makes you smile?

I might be walking down the street feeling totally neutral. As soon as I glance a kid, my face lights up—I feel a smile so deep within me. Children are my most direct way to a smile. They fascinate me. Can't take my eyes off of them. Their natural reaction to life enchants me. Of course, my work would involve children!

Much of what I write, present, and a lot of the work I do leads us back to childhood. When I started working directly with children in classrooms, I learned very quickly that they are perfect. As Dr. Montessori discovered, they come into the world as fresh spirits embodying the very best in us. They arrive with the most open heart, passionate about life, trusting it all. They are our reminder of the way to a better world. What we see and love in them is our own beauty reflected back at us.

We come into the world very clear on what makes us smile.

What makes you smile? Note them, remember them, embrace them.

These smiles are our road to bliss. As Joseph Campbell said, "Follow your bliss and the universe will open doors for you where there were only walls."

Divine Timing

There is a perfection to the timing of our life. Believe it or not, you are exactly where you are supposed to be, doing exactly what you are doing right now: Reading this book! Truth is life knows exactly what we need every step of the way. And even, especially, the tougher moments offer some of the best gifts along the journey. By trusting life implicitly and being very present to the moment, we show up as our best self and from there, life takes care of the details.

Say we're in a job we don't love, and we know what makes our heart sing, and we're feeling frustrated and stuck right now. Chances are we're going to linger on in that space for a while. If, on the other hand, we say "OK Life, I must be here for a reason, I'm open to learning from this experience, use me for *Your Highest good.*" In an instant, we'll get it, the reason we are there and very promptly, showing up at our best, the equation will shift. Maybe, we might actually start enjoying being there! And at about that moment, the next opportunity comes up. Better suited to a better us.

Life is always on our side. There are no setbacks. Only opportunities to learn more and grow more and become more loving every step of the way. That is essentially why we are here. That is all we will take away with us. The love we give and the love we receive. *A Course in Miracles* teaches that "Miracles occur naturally as expressions of love. The real miracle is the love that inspires them." When we look at life from that perspective, remembering only the love, the past will no longer hold us back. We will live the moment, showing up for the present.

Abundance

How abundant are you? Seriously. This is a serious question. Some people have a lot of money and yet they feel poor. Some people have $20 in their pocket and they are abundant! How does that work? They seem to have all that they need every moment that they need it. It just shows up. Miraculously.

Abundance is an inside job. When we feel prosperous from the inside out, we manifest all sorts of abundance. Do you feel prosperous with time, with love, with beauty, with kindness, with fun, with delicious food? Because what's the point really of having lots of money and being poor in time or love or delicious everything? That kind of abundance slips right out of our hands. Somewhere deep inside, we don't feel we deserve it, so it goes . . . On health issues, wrong deals, poor choices.

When we love ourselves, respecting our spirit, filling our life with what feels good, looking after our health, pacing ourselves, we tend to make better choices for ourselves and for the world. Happy people making the world a happier place. That's the motto. As we tend to our well-being, our influence grows. Others want to know how we do it and our world expands as a result. We are inspired and inspiring. When we are true to ourselves and to what feels good to us, we find ourselves in a position where we are able to help others.

Love Energy

It's quite funny sometimes when I'm listening to someone tell me "there's too much going on at work right now, I don't have time for love."

Separating the two is impossible. Because unless our work is imbued with love, it won't get off the ground. It just won't. Lots of false starts, minor deals maybe—but it won't flow and lead to the true abundance we're craving. "Work is love made visible" wrote Khalil Gibran. That is the essence of it.

And love can't be categorised. It's a whole. It is love energy which goes into every aspect of our life. We can't keep the door closed on one corner and expect it to shine in another area. Not possible. Just not possible.

Love is love is love is love. Unless we are feeling it in every part of our existence, life will jam bits and pieces until we understand that truth.

Love is energy. It creates miracles. It is the power.

Love is your power

Notice that feeling you have when in certain shops or with certain people. You just like the feeling. You end buying more or floating around the shop longer and end up buying more anyway . . . Or just wanting to be around that energy. It's the same with products, we are drawn to certain products more than to others. They might be identical in description, yet we just want to buy one over the other. That's energy! The energy within the shop. The energy of the person. The energy that went into creating the product.

It's the same with people. Some people might say odd things but we like them anyway. And others might be saying or doing all the right things and intuitively we're just not drawn. Maya Angelou noted that "people will forget what you said, people will forget what you did, but people will never forget how you made them feel." That's energy.

When we wake up in the morning and hand the day over to the universe praying that we be used for its highest good, we carry that energy with us. It's the *give* energy and it's also the *receive* energy. When our only goal is that our hands, our feet, our words, our deeds be used in the service of love, miracles happen.

So remember, it's never *Sales*, it's *Service*.

And by the way, it's the same for relationships. Love energy is magnetic.

Fun

In one of my after school classes, I was introducing a make-a-word puzzle to a four year old. I could feel he was exhausted after a full day at school and I was beginning to rethink this work. He suddenly noticed the egg timer in the box. His fascination over this discovery became the trigger. He wanted to beat the egg timer to completing the task every time. It was so interesting to me that this extra bit of stimulation was able to offer this boy energy and enthusiasm. It completely changed the vibe of the work. He was now enthralled. At the end of class, he asked me if he could borrow it and take it home until the next class. A week later, I saw his mother who shared with me her son's utter delight with the egg timer. She said he was using it for everything: getting dressed, brushing his teeth, eating his breakfast. She said that he was on a mission!

How simple, to introduce an element of fun to tasks that we want children to undertake. They are practicing completion and are motivated to excel. This particular child found the speed element pleasing. Another may enjoy singing whilst clearing up. Another may enjoy dancing. The point is to find the fun. We all need fun in our everyday activities. It has been proven that people who take dance breaks in the midst of work are happier, healthier and fitter!

Resistance

What we resist the most will keep coming back until we stop resisting it. In fact, the universe wants us to say "Yes" and go with the flow. By going with the flow, the universe offers exactly what we need for our journey. We feel abundant. We live trusting that everything is happening for our highest good. When we resist, the lesson keeps coming at us, until we "get" it!

Sometimes, I'm in class and I want to read a super interesting book to the children. I've been planning this. I found the book, ordered it, waited for its arrival and here we are—ready at last. The children's energy is hyped up. They're struggling to stay still. I'm trying everything I know to have their attention, it just ain't working. I could raise my voice and in an authoritarian way, order their attention. I would have broken their will because that is what I think would be good for them.

How about I say Yes to the universe and we all get up. Putting the book aside, it might have another moment. For now, what are these kids after? They want to move and laugh and do yoga poses. What's so wrong with that? In the end, I'm laughing with them. I'm working with the energy that's around me. I know that movement is good for their brain development and I know that laughter is medicine for life. How can any of this not be right? I had a lesson in mind but the universe had another! The path of least resistance is always the best.

And you know what the bonus was? After they finished their yoga positions, they sat down ready for the book—on their own. It was their choice to discover the lesson now. Reading will not be a drag in the future. When they were ready to learn, the teacher appeared. Their brains were now open to take in that information. Their bodies needed to move first. Just like our brains are in better shape when we are fit and healthy. At that point, their little bodies needed to move. In the way of the Tao, it's about *going with the flow*.

Seven Year Cycles

Scientists have discovered that it takes our cells about seven years to regenerate. As Alisa Vitti puts it, "Since on a cellular level you're a new person every seven years, the genetic material manufactured from that cell turnover sets you up for a future of thriving or nosediving."

Life essentially moves in seven year cycles. The first of these, zero to seven, opens up the gateways of so much that we absorb from our environments. It is the peak of language learning and subconsciously taking in the many messages we hear around us.

The seven year cycles continue throughout life. It's as if we have big forks in the road at these seven year junctures: 7, 14, 21, 28 and so on. Big decisions are needed. Major choices to be made. The sooner we branch off following the energy, exercising our courageous heart, trusting life, the gentler it all gets. Say we have a choice at 35 to stay numb and safe or take a major risk in pursuing what feels good. If we fork out in the direction of the heart, life joins in and supports us along the way. If we ignore that signpost, we'll hang in there for another seven years, watching it all get even tougher, and then we'll have another choice to make. The choices become tougher and tougher with the passage of time. So the sooner we follow our heart and start dancing with life, the sooner the satisfaction begins.

It's ultimately all about connecting back to our truth. Back to the question of who we are and what makes us come alive.

Health

"Health is inner peace."

A Course in Miracles

One night as I was falling asleep, I felt a bruise around my ankle. Over the next few days, my ankle swelled up and I wondered what was going on. My first reaction was to reach for Louise Hay's book *You Can Heal Your Life* in an effort to understand the thought pattern that might have lead to this. Sure enough, the probable cause was linked to guilt. She writes "Ankles represent the ability to receive pleasure." Exactly what had been going on with me for the last few weeks. For the first time, my only mission was to write. What I love doing. For the first time ever in my life, everyone around me supported what I loved and wanted to do. And here I was feeling guilty if I let a minute pass without actually being in front of the computer, writing.

I forgot about everything I was actually creating. What we love is what we are here to do. When one sits down to write, we are actually putting our life into words. Our life goes into our creation. They are not separate. So my feeling guilty about doing anything other than writing could not be more counterproductive. The guilt made the situation worse in that I actually didn't feel like writing much. It started to feel like an obligation, a chore. All the pleasure and fun that usually has me on a roll was depleted. All of a sudden I couldn't understand that this, that I wanted to do more than anything else, and finally with the support of those I love, became a drag. Surreal, right? So my body revolted and brought out the physical symptom for guilt and my not allowing all the pleasure life was trying to deliver.

I had to remember that it was about more than just writing a book. I was really sharing my love with the world. That is what the reader would feel in absorbing the words. It's all about the energy that goes into the creation. That is what we tap into when we choose a product, a service and so on. Knowing all this intellectually, life now ensured that I exercised my knowledge. No, a book coming out of obligation was not going to cut it. This book was emanating from my heart and going out into the world with that energy. And until I was ready to dance with life again, to have fun while creating, it was *no systems go*. As soon as I got it, a few affirmations along the lines of "I deserve to rejoice in life. I accept all the pleasure life has to offer" and I was back on track . . . Writing from the heart.

Kids & Food

Sometimes, I feel like a spokesperson for children. This is one of them. Often when I'm walking home, I will notice children in the three to six year age group with a huge sweet thing in their hand—an ice cream, a candy bar or the like. Over Easter recently, one of my best friends' daughters offloaded her full pockets of chocolate eggs to me. I was surprised and asked her why she was giving them all to me. Her answer was "I don't like chocolate!" in French. How often do we hear that from kids?! Or from anyone for that matter. Chocolate is addictive. The more we eat it, the more we crave it. I was not a big chocolate person and could go for months not eating any. I notice, however, that if I do eat something chocolaty at say 4pm. Sure enough, at 4pm the next day, I will feel like eating chocolate again. I would have to consciously break the habit. I'm an adult and I know how to do that.

The reason my friend's daughter doesn't like chocolate is because she doesn't really know chocolate. She is given raisins to nibble on. Children can become chocolate addicts. They will literally have withdrawal symptoms and can get quite moody and annoying if not given the chocolate. That's scary. I know numerous research articles have emerged about the benefits of chocolate. Everything in moderation. It's not about depriving ourselves of any food. Any attempt at that, would make the missing link the top craving! Sometimes, after holidays, when we have sampled too many delicious things, our system will want a period of lighter foods. I believe our bodies know exactly what we need and if it is a piece of chocolate, then so be it. But why would we want to encourage an addiction at such a young age, when children don't know better, when children still need our guidance.

I believe that we become junk foodies because we grow up eating junk food. I ate a Mediterranean diet as a child and now when I'm hungry, I tend to crave real food. And if my only option is something sweet or junky, I'll wait for the real thing. It just won't feel satisfying until I eat something relatively substantial. It's all about the early habits we establish in children's lives. Input is output. What we put into our body is the fuel. Let children know what it feels like to be healthy. They will then detect a difference when they are reaching for the junk.

In discussing food, I feel a need to add the importance of children eating a lot. Children need food for their brains and bodies to grow. Sometimes, when we battle with weight issues ourselves, we tend to pass on that anxiety to children, albeit unconsciously. It is important to remember that children need to eat—and a lot. Eating what they feel like, within a healthy exposure, is the recipe! If they want a third serving of rice and chicken— why not? That's great. Better they fill up on that, than a useless dessert. Let the fridge and cupboards offer everything healthy. That way, whatever they reach for will be good stuff.

In a fascinating experiment conducted in the 1930s, scientists gave a group of children open access to a buffet with every kind of food, from desserts to green vegetables. They were allowed to eat whatever they felt like for thirty days. It turned out that by the end of the research period, every child had eaten the right proportion of every food group, making up the healthy food triangle. Like everything else, our bodies know best what we need and when. This is the foundation of intuitive eating with which we are all primed.

Sleep

Children need almost twelve hours sleep when their brains and bodies are growing rapidly. So often, I come across children who are exhausted. I mean they are literally falling asleep all over the place. Children definitely reach an age when they don't want to go to sleep. They somehow feel like they're missing out on something. A lot of times, when over-exhausted, they start operating on hyper adrenalin and may have a new burst of energy. From there, if we insist and are a little strict about getting them into bed, they fall asleep almost immediately. They are literally operating on a second wind, which at that age, is not sustainable. They don't know better. They will thank you later on in life when they realise how healthy they were as children.

How about we make sleeping fun? Reminding them that they will grow overnight—taller, smarter, cuter, funnier! Joyce Dunbar's book *Shoe Baby* really hones in on that message. And sometimes children are afraid of the dark. Their imagination takes them to strange places where the radiator's clanking sounds like monsters. It's fascinating because just a year later, they themselves will remember how certain things scared them and they would have outgrown them naturally. The idea here is to soothe them. Children enjoy prayer, and what a lovely habit to start early on. The idea that angels are watching over them as they sleep. Children's prayers are magical in the goodness they are always wishing for everyone. Wave to the moon and say goodnight to the stars. Let's make the sleeping ritual an event. That's a habit worth keeping!

Reflecting

Socrates said "The unexamined life is not worth living." It all begins with observation. As one observes a child, one learns. We learn about human nature, we learn about development but most important, we learn about the child. Play is a huge window into what later becomes self-analysis.

I had a child in one of my classes who was the eldest at three. She had a two year old sister and the mother was pregnant with another child en route. This child came from a bilingual home and was learning English as a third language through KidsMeridian. The mother explained to me that her daughter was not speaking at school but would speak non-stop to her. The mother also explained that the younger sister was the life and soul of all gatherings whilst the eldest was rather shy and held back. As we got to know each other over the first few sessions, this child did not talk. She was engaged in activities and clearly quite happy in the environment. Eventually, she took my hand, explained that I was now the baby and guided me to a corner. She asked me to sit down, she made believe to put tape on my mouth so I would not talk. She then taped my eyes so I wouldn't see and then my hands and feet so I wouldn't move. I was then placed in the fridge with the door shut. She wanted to make believe this scene for months. It was clear that the baby talking and moving was not what she wanted. I assumed the baby to be the younger sister and maybe even the baby coming up. She obviously was not enjoying being in the background as the *baby* would take over the show. Through play, she was giving me some very important information. This information was highly useful in my understanding her language progress. This information, however, is even more important at the personal analysis level.

At such a young age, the issues are so natural and obvious to discern. Later on in life, we learn to mask them consciously or unconsciously. Ultimately, we all want to be understood. If we encourage that self-understanding from the youngest instant, we encourage children to continue to be true to their feelings. This truth is their instinct, their intuition. It is this guiding force that leads us to do great things with our life. It is this truth that we will look back on when we reflect on our life. So, watch closely. Play, ask for feedback on films they are watching, books they are reading. Ask them to tell you stories. Ask them to explain their drawings—once finished. This is a very important point. It is best not to ask a child what he is going to draw, paint, build and so on. Best to let them get on with it, and only when they have finished or are satisfied with their work, do we then proceed to discuss with them their thoughts and feelings. Many times, one doesn't know in advance what one is creating. It is best to let the flow take care of the direction. What we want to understand is the essence of the messages.

"I have no use for this"

A Course in Miracles explains that when we are ready to be healed the message is "I have no use for this." What happens very often is that illness strikes as a way for us to come to terms with what we are really feeling. It's life's way of getting our attention. Our willingness to understand the lesson behind it and our desire for true healing is all it takes for the healing to occur. Our willingness brings to us the answers. A book lands in our hands, our intuition leads us to buy a certain magazine or to call someone who happens to say just what we need to hear. The message for the solution is unveiled very promptly when we are genuinely open to knowing.

This is where Louise Hay's work is genius. She connects every *dis-ease* with the probable cause. Since all disorders stem from our thoughts, the body just manifests whatever it is we are feeling that is not in line with our truth. It is the weak way of expressing something going on within us. Our spirit is strong. We are strong since we are spirits inhabiting a physical body. It really doesn't matter how weak the body is . . . Once our spirit remembers its power, the healing is immediate. Illness often allows us to do what we really want to do. As in, we really don't feel like going to work, suddenly we have the flu and we're home. Once we understand that there is another way to express our truth, we have no need for dis-ease any more.

Love is always the answer. *A Course in Miracles* teaches that only love is real. All else is illusion. And that is the truth. When we are not loving ourselves enough, when we have forgotten about our truth, our power, we feel victim to the world. In fact, we are completely creating the world we live in. All the situations we find ourselves in, our soul has manoeuvred to bring us back on track. There is a plan, and it's a great one. And unless we're on that path, we're going to have a few bumps along the way to steer us back in the right direction. It's all about coming back to love. "Love love love. That is the soul of genius" said Mozart, and how right was he!

It is in loving ourselves, respecting what feels good to our spirit and moving along in that direction, that life flows. That's where the big line comes from: "Follow your heart." Our heart will always win in the end. And if it has to incapacitate us along the way to remind us who we are and why we are here, it will do that. Better we catch the messages along the way. And at the slight nudging, take action. The body is just in service to our spirit's feelings.

So these bodies which kindly carry that big powerful spirit of ours through the lifetime have to be loved and respected. Why wait for an issue to remember how lucky we are to be healthy? Even if we are trying to lose weight or getting over a burn, whatever is going on physically, a huge appreciation for the work our body does is called for. The hands that allow us to know the world, the legs that carry us from place to place, and sometimes in very high heels! The digestion that takes in all we eat, the skin that stays soft and healthy. Every single part of us needs love. So when we're in the shower or we have a moment, let's always remember that this body is so important in the work it allows our spirit to create. Focusing on all the good that is there is vital. Even in the midst of an ailment, appreciation of its normal functioning pronounced from the heart is so very powerful. The idea is to see it already healed.

After a few days of swelling, I wanted to just be over with it. I felt I truly understood the message and was feeling such gratitude for my perfect health. I knew as a child of God, I deserved all my good and that in sharing everything I had learned I was truly doing the work I came here to do. My intuition reminded me of a meditation I had come across on healing. It was Dr. Brian Weiss' *Enlightenment and Healing through Meditation*. One of the most soothing meditations I have ever come across. If anyone has anything going on health-wise, this is really worth discovering.

I was led to see my osteopath thinking I must have also strained my ankle. It turned out I had to revamp my nutrition, get back to yoga and cry out a few remaining bits as I was bringing my book to life. All that I had learned in my journey so far had to be revisited, from a deeper place. I had always been fascinated by our body's self-correcting abilities. As a teenager, I had read a lot about the power of nutrition and herbs to heal. I had always been very healthy, choosing organic, exercising regularly. For some reason, I had recently taken all that for granted. Being back in London, I was on a Marmite diet, craving it night and day. And it had been a particularly cold winter and I, being an introvert by nature, was relishing home time, above exercise too. Oh my, everything I believed in was being tested here.

My swollen ankle also made it quite painful sitting for long periods of time at the computer. Clever life! I had to get up and move regularly. Plus, it allowed me to think about the book with distance. I was now working from inspiration again. The moment I uttered "I have no use for this," I was brought back to life. In every sense. Here I was writing a book on tapping into miracles. What would be the point of creating a great book and not being in optimal health to enjoy it?!

Surrender

"Certain thoughts are prayers.
There are moments when,
whatever be the attitude of the body,
the soul is on its knees."

Victor Hugo

*T*he ego sees surrender as an act of weakness, when letting go actually musters up all our strength. There is a grace that accompanies the process of release. It's the moment when all the control in the world can't fix it, or solve it, or even figure it out. It's the moment we say 'Ok universe, over to you.' When we know at the deepest level of our being that we have tried our best, used up every resource known to man, when we have exhausted our logical mind . . . This is when we discover that there is another way. And the other way is actually so much easier. It's almost like life waits for us to surrender the plans we have for ourselves before it can show us what it has in mind. And the divine plan is always so much more compelling. Not to mention how much more gentle it is to access. It's easy, it's guided, it's magnificent. It is beautiful.

When we are open, asking to be shown the way, every door will open. Books will drop off shelves onto our lap. People will line up to help. Opportunities just start showing up. We're in the right place at the right time. And we are open. Ready to receive. It's like a dance with life. So good. Feels like music.

Joseph Campbell noted that "We must let go of the life we have planned, so as to accept the one that is waiting for us." We have to be willing to give up the life we planned in order to receive what life has in mind for us. This is not saying we are not receiving exactly what we want. It's just that the process is different. Picture a woman madly in love with a man. She lets herself go, forgets about her plans and what she really wants. She's thinking it's him she wants. That's it, just him. On any terms. If she succeeds with this scenario, the feeling will always be that he did her a favour by giving in. Like she convinced him to be with her. How unsexy.

Fast forward the scenario. She tries everything. Seduction and all. She just doesn't quite make it. She throws her hands up in the air. Enough is enough. She gets busy getting back on track. Her passion is reignited. And yes, he still lingers on in her heart. But her passion is bigger than him, bigger than her. She's lit up from the inside out. Gorgeously sexy woman is now not just that, but a magnet for all her good. Things line up. As she lives on purpose, life delivers everything she needs. It's like magic. She thinks of something and there it is. She hasn't even had a chance to add it to her list yet, it just shows up. The thoughts are so powerful. Life is conspiring to guide her and get her there. Her spirit is on a roll. It's rock & roll time in her life. She feels more and more filled up from the inside out. She's glowing, her eyes are twinkling. She knows this is it. This is the journey she really came here to live.

And guess what, Mr. Intuition shows up now. How different is this scenario? As far as she's concerned, she has her groove back. She's dancing with life!

Faith

Abraham Lincoln said "I have been driven many times upon my knees by the overwhelming conviction that I had no where else to go. My own wisdom and that of all about me seemed insufficient for that day." Call it Higher power, source, inner guidance, angels, spirit— You name it. In Star Wars, it's "The Force" is within *You!* The point is simply that this energy moves mountains. It begins as a mustard seed of hope and leads us to the top.

When we are aligned with that power, our energy is of a higher vibration. It's almost like we're working on behalf of the universe. And with that, the co-creation is easy. Only we, in the format of our life and experience, can contribute our bit to the divine plan. It's very specific. No two people ever match in terms of their exact offering. This is why each individual is so important in the big picture. This is why it's a divine plan. Our contribution is part of the puzzle. When we are adding our piece, we know it. It's so completely obvious to our whole being. Finally, we're back on track. You see, there is a plan and our soul knows exactly what it is. And when we are not moving in that direction, we feel it. Something feels off. And nothing on the outside of us can ever complete the void inside. Not the perfect mate, not the money, not all the fame in the world. And you know the rest—workaholic, alcoholic, chocoholic, shopaholic, etc are all very short term bandaids for a deep emptiness that is begging to be filled.

Showing up as our best self

True integrity is who we are when no one is watching. It's not a performance. It's our truth. When we live from that place where we are doing the very best we can, we know it. It doesn't mean we have to be perfect all the time. It just means that we are striving to live a life that feels good at the deepest level of our being.

As Abraham Lincoln said, "When I do good, I feel good. When I do bad, I feel bad. That is my religion." How perfect is that? And how true. We know when we've done good. We feel the universe thanking us! That is the feeling of true joy. We feel so filled up from the inside out. Nothing can replace that feeling. True satisfaction of the soul. When we discover that feeling, we understand why we are here.

Giving

In order for our life to make sense, we need to feel that we make a difference. In contribution, we feel a sense of purpose. Our life must therefore have a higher purpose and that is to be of service. No matter how much we accumulate in success, material or otherwise, we will always feel a void, something within us that can't be filled up properly. A satisfaction missing. It is in creating a higher purpose, in giving, that we find peace.

Sometimes, we are thinking big scale in terms of contribution and therefore never know how to get started. Feeling we can't possibly make such a difference. The key is to start small. Your own circle probably needs more love and patience. The supermarket teller would appreciate a kind vibe, so would the next door car on the motor way. Look around and be love today. Starting is the way to contribution. We feel better and better each day, and more and more powerful every moment.

Children are sometimes given so much, in terms of toys and things. Yet, they look unsatisfied. We need to give to feel really good. Since children are so intuitive, they can feel something is off with that equation. When we re-energise them with the help they want to give, we have happy children. When they are involved in preparing a Thanksgiving meal for the homeless or making a card for someone ill, they feel nourished and at peace.

That feeling of service will stay with them forever, they will know what truly nourishes the soul. It's not the latest gadget. No amount of gadget-collecting will get us there. It's in the giving. Start today. Just look around and start giving—love, thank yous, your time, your gentleness, your warmth. Give from your heart. Give money and feel abundant. The more you give, the more you receive. That's how it works.

Spirituality

It is said that religion is for those who are afraid of hell and spirituality is for those who have already been there.

In the olden days, we had chapels in our gardens and we would go there to talk to God. Then, formalised religion created an in-between interpreter. If it makes you happy to go to the formal House to commune with Higher Power, then great. If however, we want to be in touch with our inner guidance at all times, then we might have to create our own practice.

Maria Montessori set up little chapels in the classrooms where children might go, light a candle and sit in silence. The corner offered a great deal of self-mastering challenges for children. Moving chairs gently, lighting the candle carefully and sitting in silence is also quite an effort for kids. The ritual in itself offers a lot. It is the *House of God* and everyone is welcome at anytime they feel like visiting. It is a moment to check in with one's heart. To quiet the mind and regroup. I think it's quite magical and may be re-instated in any format since religion is ultimately about love. Love is within us all.

Our own altar might be a certain bench in the park or a huge cushion that we love. The important thing is just that we feel soothed there. My favourite prayers have taken place under starry starry nights in the midst of lavender and roses. I'm in heaven in those moments. Whatever place or feeling takes you there is your altar.

It might be looking at your child's face, sitting in a bubble bath, in the midst of Mother Nature, savouring a home-cooked meal just concocted.

According to *A Course in Miracles*, "To be in the Kingdom is merely to focus your full attention on it." Spirituality is the experience of feeling God every second of the day, with every encounter, every smile . . . In the flowers, in the beauty, in the love.

Tap into Miracles

A Course in Miracles reminds us that "Miracles are natural. When they do not occur something has gone wrong."

Let's visualise it. Imagine a tap. Imagine water flowing beautifully, clearly, easily through that tap. Now imagine this tap is suddenly only dripping water, its flow is somehow obstructed. It is temperamental, unpredictable and just annoying. Much like with that tap, our life is supposed to flow—easily, healthily and abundantly. When the flow is choppy, complicated and unclear, the tap is clogged.

What would clog the tap? Unnecessary bits from the past stuck in there. Same with us, we might be holding on to resentments and disappointments gathered along the way. Our past is holding back the natural flow now. When we let go those situations that are taking up space, universal energy is able to support our healthy movement forward. In cleaning out the tap, we allow energy to flow freely again.

When we feel love and appreciation, miracles abound. When we hold on to resentments and grievances, we hold back the flow. The energy is stuck. When we forgive, we release our energy to move towards our magnificent life. A life filled with what we love. What we love begins to appreciate. And as we appreciate it more and more, it appreciates more and more . . . And the tap is flowing abundantly again!

Forgiveness is a big word and often brings with it the idea that certain events and circumstances are difficult to forgive. The point to remember here is that the willingness to forgive is all it takes. That willingness alone invites spirit to create the circumstances for the forgiveness to occur. And this willingness is what releases the energy that is stuck, to flow freely again, leading us back to the miraculous life we are here to live.

And the forgiveness is not just for others. Forgiving ourselves is just as important. The key here is to remember that every step along the way constitutes part of the learning. We are here to remember our truth, who we really are. The child who came into the world filled with love and only love. When things don't work out along the way, we are just being guided to go deeper in remembering that truth. When we learn to accept the perfection of it all, knowing that every piece is a necessary part of the journey, our hearts open. Trusting life invites the good. Every disappointment becomes a blessing in disguise when we are ready to learn and grow.

Life is supposed to be easy and joyful and abundant, in every way. At our deepest core, we know that. We might even remember moments in our life when life really supported us and everything flowed. If we remember our state of mind then, we will remember that we were in sync with our hearts and as a result, the energy was vibrant.

So it's time to clear the tap and let go of the past. It's time to embrace the present. That's why it's called the *Present*! Let's discover together the gifts that life holds when our energy is aligned with love and beauty and miracles. As Albert Einstein realised, "There are only two ways to live your life. One is as though nothing is a miracle. The other is as though everything is a miracle."

The Dance

Life becomes the employer, the banker, the match-maker, the estate agent . . . Everything. When we know what we want and have unwavering faith in life's delivery, we live from a place of trust. We trust the timing, we trust the methodology, we trust our dance partner!

When we know that life is for us and that any delay along the way is just ensuring that we are ready to receive, we live expecting miracles. We know that life understands our needs, our wants, our desires. And that these are, in fact, God's whispers to our heart. This is the life we are here to live, to experience, to share.

And from that place, we live our most inspired and inspiring life. We experience life as a dance. We move, we flow, we rejoice in the music, in the moment, in the beauty.

I wish you the dance of a lifetime . . .

Afterword

Believe nothing,
no matter where you read it
or who has said it,
not even if I have said it,
unless it agrees with
your own reason and
your own common sense.

~Buddha

What I'm about to say next might be quite new as a concept for some of you. Just entertain the idea for now. You'll decide later if it makes sense to you or not.

If we believe in God, the Universe, our Higher purpose—you choose the name—we could not possibly imagine how a good God would allow a helpless baby to be born to an abusive family. The only way such an injustice would make sense is if the soul selected the specific family for lessons to be learned in this lifetime. As spirits, we are eternal. The way I see it, when we are done with what we have to do on the physical plane, we simply go to the light. This is what research offers from those who have had near death experiences. My feeling is that we then sit with angels, and review our life by observing it objectively—like watching a movie! From there, we decide how we did and the lessons we would like to take on next.

Kahlil Gibran expresses it so beautifully, "A little while, a moment of rest upon the wind, and another woman shall bear me." Essentially, I believe that we choose our family based on kick-starting our soul's journey. We may be here to learn patience or anger-management or empathy. The thing is, somewhere in childhood, we forget what we are here for. Usually, whatever has been our toughest lesson to date is the link to what we are here to learn. So, if we've been struggling with relationships for instance, then this is probably an area in which we have much to contribute. Think about it, if you were trying to loose weight, would you rather hear about it from someone who has never had a weight issue, someone who was born with a *speedy gonzales* metabolism, someone who is a natural outdoorsy athletic type? Wouldn't you rather talk to someone who has been battling with it their whole life, going up and down the scales . . . Someone who may also have grown up in a family where this was an issue and it might have just been passed on?

We break the cycle when we change our karma, when we say "Stop, that's enough. There is another way and I'm going to figure it out." In Thomas A. Edison's words, "There's a way to do it better—Find it." That is the end of that cycle and the lesson would have been properly mastered in this lifetime. A child born into an alcoholic family may initially be a big drinker too. The soul will then force the issue. Something major will ensue, an accident of some sort. The alcoholic will then address the issue and may choose to spend his life teaching others about it.

They say that the best way to overcome karmic debt is to forgive. So, that is what we do, we forgive those who taught us our big lessons. I bet if you consider this, you will see exactly where your lessons were kick-started. We might not be aware of it until much later on in life. When we are ready, we realise why we chose specific situations. In fact, if we change our take on the problems in life, and think of them as our lessons, we will stay awake to our growth. The key is be aware. It is so easy to be asleep for a big part of one's life, complaining. You know the song, everything is difficult and complicated. And on and on it goes . . . We all know what that's like! Actually life is not meant to be tough. It is meant to flow. When we encounter the tougher moments, we have to get to the bottom of them. When we try to understand what life is teaching us, we're back in gentle territory again.

So the question is, "What's the lesson here?"

"There is no world apart from what you wish, and herein lies your ultimate release. Change but your mind on what you want to see, and all the world must change accordingly."

A Course in Miracles

Inspiring Books

"I don't believe people are looking
for the meaning of life
as much as they are looking for the
experience of being alive."

Joseph Campbell

The Answer is Simple—Sonia Choquette
The Alchemist—Paulo Coelho
A Deep Breath of Life, How Good Can It Get?
　　—Alan Cohen
The 7 Habits of Highly Effective People—Stephen Covey
The Circle—Laura Day
The 21-day Consciousness Cleanse—Debbie Ford
Creative Visualization, Creating True Prosperity
　　—Shakti Gawain
The Prophet—Kahlil Gibran
You Can Heal Your Life—Louise L. Hay
Giving the Love that Heals—Harville Hendrix
Feel the Fear and Do It Anyway—Susan Jeffers
The Fire Starter Sessions—Danielle LaPorte
The Absorbent Mind, The Discovery of the Child,
　　The Secret of Childhood—Dr. Maria Montessori
Why Me, Why This, Why now?—Robin Norwood
Much More than the ABCs—Judith A. Schickedanz
The Game of Life and How to Play It—Florence Scovel
　　Shinn
WomanCode—Alisa Vitti
Same Soul Many Lives—Dr. Brian Weiss
Infinite Self—Stuart Wilde
A Return to Love, Enchanted Love, Illuminata
　　—Marianne Williamson

For Kids

The Littlest Matryoshka—Corinne Bliss
The Fourth Little Pig—Teresa Celsi
Shoe Baby—Joyce Dunbar
A Little Princess—Frances Hodgson Burnett
Drawing Book of Faces—Ed Emberley
Amazing Grace—Mary Hoffman
How to Catch a Star—Oliver Jeffers
Be a Friend to Trees—Patricia Lauber
The Paper Bag Princess—Robert Munsch
The Three Questions—Jon J. Muth
The Peace Book—Todd Parr
Le Petit Prince—Antoine de Saint-Exupéry
The Giving Tree—Shel Silverstein
Joseph had a Little Overcoat—Simms Taback
Thank You Angels—Doreen Virtue
A Red-Riding Hood Story from China—Ed Young

& Teens

Girlosophy—Anthea Paul
The Secret—Rhonda Byrne

Music

"My future starts when I wake up every morning . . .
Every day I find something creative
to do with my life."

Miles Davis

**The music that played and played,
inspiring this creation!**

Tidal—Fiona Apple
We Have All the Time in the World—Louis Armstrong
Verse—Patricia Barber
Leap of Faith—Bluey
Kind of Blue, Tutu—Miles Davis
Deleted Scenes from the Cutting Room Floor—Caro Emerald
My One and Only Thrill, The Absence—Melody Gardot
Gifts of the Angels—Steven Halpern
Girl on Fire—Alicia Keys
The John Lennon Collection
Legend—Bob Marley
True to Myself—Ziggy Marley
The Truth About Love—Pink
Soldier of Love—Sade
Best of The Best—Sinatra
Buying Time—Miss 600
Blue Note Plays Sting
Songs from Kahlil Gibran's The Prophet—Sarah Warwick

Some Montessori Alumni

Google founders Larry Page and Sergey Brin credit much of their success to their going to Montessori school! And here are a few other notables . . .

Jeff Bezos, founder Amazon.com
Joshua Bell, violinist, owner of Stradivarius violin
Julia Child, chef, star of TV cooking shows
Jacqueline Bouvier Kennedy Onassis, former editor and First Lady
Gabriel Garcia Marquez, Nobel Prize winner for Literature
Friedensreich Hundertwasser, Austrian painter and architect
Jimmy Wales, founder of Wikipedia
Helen Hunt, Academy Award-winning actress
George Clooney, Academy Award-winning actor
Will Wright, designer of The Sims
Katharine Graham, former owner-editor the Washington Post
Anne Frank, famous diarist from world War II
Sean "P. Diddy" Coombs, rap star and music mogul
Prince William and Prince Harry, British Royal Family

Montessori Supporters:

Erik Erikson, anthropologist/author, had a Montessori
    teaching certification
Jean Piaget, Psychologist, conducted child observations
    in a Montessori school
Alexander Graham Bell, inventor, provided financial
    support to Dr. Montessori
Thomas Edison, scientist and inventor, founded a
    Montessori school
Mahatma Gandhi hosted Dr. Montessori during her
    years in India
President Wilson's daughter trained as a Montessori
    teacher. A Montessori classroom was set up in the
    White House during Wilson's presidency!

Acknowledgements

"If the only prayer you ever say in your entire life is
thank you,
it will be enough."

Meister Eckhart

So many thank yous

My first thank you goes to my very beautiful mother. Thank you for bringing me into the world. Without you, none of this would be possible. It was your vision that opened up so many wonderful educational opportunities for me. Thank you for igniting in me a fascination for languages, people and the sunny side of life! Thank you to my wonderful father whose love and support I feel at the deepest level of my being. Your passion for delicious food, luxurious travel and good story-telling are with me for life now. Thank you to my amazing brother for being the techie in the family and for setting all of us up. Don't know how I would have ever gotten started without you saying "that's it, it's going live now!"

I especially want to thank my big sister Karen Angelini for being, as her name implies, an angel in my life. I am convinced we are soul family and I was placed next to "the imperial suite" at Wellesley for that reason! Thank you for listening to me from your heart, for knowing me and encouraging me every step of the way. Thank you for your belief in this work, your unwavering support, your patient re-reads and genius edits. I feel so blessed to have you in my life.

I come from a long line of very inspiring men and women. Grandfathers, grandmothers, great grandparents and aunties! The next thank you is for Didi, my divinely gorgeous youngest aunt. Being with you in your 'little house on the prairie' was so important for my spirit. Thank you for the inspiration, the support and the soul food you provided. Know that I feel the appreciation in every cell of my being.

Thank you to my magical cousins who have all been there at such important stages of my life—From wonderful Thanksgivings to cozy Hong Kong typhoons to fun vortex moments!

Thank you to my friends, my treasures in this lifetime. Thank you Kerstin Roolfs for reminding me that I am an artist! And for helping me bring this book to life. It was through our conversations that I finally understood the work I am here to do. I am so happy to have had a chance to share the WB loft with you. As the man said, we are "sisters." Thank you to Sarai Assouline—Through knowing you, the way you care, the way you live, the way you mother your magical daughters, I have learned so much. Proof that there are no mistakes in life. I worked in finance so I would meet you at DB! Thank you to Sandrine Durand. Wow, where do I begin thanking you? My very own transition coach. You are always always always there for me at such big moments in my life. Thank you life for coordinating it so perfectly for me with this angel. We have shared two of the world's most beautiful cities, NYC and Paris. It's London's turn now! Thank you Katie Tait for being a part of my life. Thank you for treating me to the best birthday gift in 2012—In writing it all down, I awakened my power and life moved mountains for me that year. Heather Gardner, from your very first sunshiny card, you continue to be a source of sunshine to me and my belongings! Thank you. Fiona Edge, we have known each other since we were seven, we have shared so much—from Bloomberg messages to Jivamukti yoga! Now clever life lets us be neighbours in London. How lucky am I? And Vasso Petrou, marketing guru and dearest friend, thank you for all your brilliant ideas—I just wasn't ready before, I am now! I would also like to thank Rainer Bormann, who sat next to me day in day out and watched me struggle with life for a moment. What you taught me turned out to be my biggest lesson in life so far. Thank you for showing me how to ask for what I want. Clearly, I have more gems in the friendship treasure chest, but this might turn into another book! Please know that every single one of you has contributed to my life and hence this book. You are all engraved in my heart.

Thank you to all the children in my life, those who have been a part of my journey so far and all the ones I have yet to meet, I can't wait! You are my greatest teachers, my deepest inspiration and my most direct way to a smile. I write for you.

And now a warm heartfelt thank you to all those who have made this book possible. Thank you to Virginia Morrel for getting me on board, and for explaining all about "Putting the baby on the bus!" And thank you to Stephanie Cornthwaite for your angelic patience. I moved cities and into a new home, amongst other things, in the midst of publishing this book. Thank you Holly Falconer for your beautiful pictures and such a fun moment in the process! And thank you Juliette Cole for looking after my health at the last integral stage of standing up, quite literally. Thank you Louise Hay for your work that heals, inspires and uplifts. I am so proud that my book is emerging with a Hay House stamp on it.

The last thank you goes to my nanny Dada who lives on in my heart. You continue to inspire me to do good every day of my life. Thank you for sharing my childhood, I feel you with me always.

To laugh often and love much;
to win the respect of intelligent persons
and the affection of children;
to earn the approbation of honest citizens
and endure the betrayal of false friends;
to appreciate beauty;
to find the best in others;
to give of one's self;
to leave the world a bit better,
whether by a healthy child,
a garden patch, or a redeemed social condition;
to have played and laughed with enthusiasm
and sung with exultation;
to know even one life has breathed
easier because you have lived—
this is to have succeeded.

Ralph Waldo Emerson

About the Author

Rania Lababidy is an inspirational speaker, a soul whisperer and a Montessorian. Her practice involves progressive work on inspiring individuals to live their truth. Remembering intrinsic interests, passions, curiosities and magnetic charisma.

Rania founded *KidsMeridian* in Paris in 2008 to support European schools in opening up to a more creative education with a focus on acquiring multiple languages in early childhood. Rania holds a Masters degree from NYU's Steinhardt School of Culture, Education and Human Development.

Rania grew up in London, attending the French Lycee and then St Paul's Girls' School. She received her B.A. from Wellesley College in International Relations and was recruited on campus to the world of investment banking. She began her finance career on Wall Street. For over a decade, she marketed the exciting growth of Asia to UK and European institutions, watching China grow from a bicycle adventure to some of the tallest, biggest and best ideas for the 21st Century. In 2004, she returned to NYC as a Director with Deutsche Bank. And, in the Big Apple, Rania remembered to follow her heart...